T0334707

SCHOENBERG: 'NIGHT MUSIC', *VERKLÄRTE NACHT* AND *ERWARTUNG*

Arnold Schoenberg (1874–1951) is often portrayed as a composer who began as a heart-on-sleeve late Romantic only to evolve during the First World War into an austere, mathematically obsessed deviser of musical puzzles. Yet to claim that in his music he replaced tonality with its absolute opposite, atonality, as the twelve-tone method swept away all trace of traditional harmonic and thematic processes, is as misleading as to argue that romantic warmth and humanity morphed into the purest and most austerely modernistic spirituality. This handbook refocuses the wealth of recent research into two of Schoenberg's major compositions; the expressive character of those relatively early works, which centre on nocturnal images of darkness and despair, is at its most original and powerful in *Verklärte Nacht* and *Erwartung*, where the dramatic interplay between stabilising continuities and disorientating fragmentations reveals the elements of a modernist aesthetics that remained fundamental to Schoenberg's musical thought.

ARNOLD WHITTALL is Professor Emeritus of Musical Theory and Analysis at King's College London. His most recent books are *The Wagner Style* (2015) and *British Music after Britten* (2020), and he is co-translator of Pierre Boulez's *Music Lessons: The Collège de France Lectures* (2018).

NEW CAMBRIDGE MUSIC HANDBOOKS

Series Editor

NICOLE GRIMES, UNIVERSITY OF CALIFORNIA, IRVINE

The New Cambridge Music Handbooks series provides accessible introductions to landmarks in music history, written by leading experts in their field. Encompassing a wide range of musical styles and genres, it embraces the music of hitherto under-represented creators as well as re-imagining works from the established canon. It will enrich the musical experience of students, scholars, listeners and performers alike.

Books in the Series

Hensel: String Quartet in E flat
Benedict Taylor

Berlioz: Symphonie Fantastique
Julian Rushton

Margaret Bonds: The Montgomery Variations and Du Bois 'Credo'
John Michael Cooper

Robert Schumann: Piano Concerto
Julian Horton

Schoenberg: 'Night Music', Verklärte Nacht and Erwartung
Arnold Whittall

Forthcoming Titles

Schubert: The 'Great' Symphony in C major
Suzannah Clark

Bach: The Cello Suites
Edward Klorman

Clara Schumann: Piano Concerto in A minor Op. 7
Julie Pedneault-Deslauriers

Donizetti: Lucia di Lammermoor
Mark Pottinger

Beethoven: String Quartet Op. 130
Elaine Sisman

Louise Farrenc: Nonet for Winds and Strings
Marie Sumner Lott

Cavalleria rusticana and Pagliacci
Alexandra Wilson

SCHOENBERG: 'NIGHT MUSIC', VERKLÄRTE NACHT AND ERWARTUNG

ARNOLD WHITTALL

King's College London

 CAMBRIDGE
UNIVERSITY PRESS

CAMBRIDGE
UNIVERSITY PRESS

Shaftesbury Road, Cambridge CB2 8EA, United Kingdom

One Liberty Plaza, 20th Floor, New York, NY 10006, USA

477 Williamstown Road, Port Melbourne, VIC 3207, Australia

314–321, 3rd Floor, Plot 3, Splendor Forum, Jasola District Centre,
New Delhi – 110025, India

103 Penang Road, #05–06/07, Visioncrest Commercial, Singapore 238467

Cambridge University Press is part of Cambridge University Press & Assessment,
a department of the University of Cambridge.

We share the University's mission to contribute to society through the pursuit of
education, learning and research at the highest international levels of excellence.

www.cambridge.org
Information on this title: www.cambridge.org/9781316514092

DOI: 10.1017/9781009082549

First published 2024

A catalogue record for this publication is available from the British Library

Library of Congress Cataloging-in-Publication Data
NAMES: Whittall, Arnold, author.
TITLE: Schoenberg : 'night music', Verklärte Nacht and Erwartung / Arnold Whittall.
DESCRIPTION: [1.] | Cambridge, United Kingdom ; New York, NY : Cambridge
University Press, 2023. | Series: New Cambridge music handbooks | Includes biblio-
graphical references and index.
IDENTIFIERS: LCCN 2023028485 (print) | LCCN 2023028486 (ebook) | ISBN
9781316514092 (hardback) | ISBN 9781009077361 (paperback) | ISBN
9781009082549 (ebook)
SUBJECTS: LCSH: Schoenberg, Arnold, 1874–1951 – Criticism and interpretation. |
Schoenberg, Arnold, 1874–1951. Verklärte Nacht. | Schoenberg, Arnold, 1874–1951.
Erwartung. | Music – 20th century – History and criticism. | Modernism (Music)
CLASSIFICATION: LCC ML410.S283 W47 2023 (print) | LCC ML410.S283 (ebook) | DDC
780.92–dc23/eng/20230620
LC record available at https://lccn.loc.gov/2023028485
LC ebook record available at https://lccn.loc.gov/2023028486

ISBN 978-1-316-51409-2 Hardback
ISBN 978-1-009-07736-1 Paperback

CONTENTS

MUSICAL EXAMPLES

PRELUDE

Historians of twentieth-century music often allot pride of place to Schoenberg's development between 1899 (when he was twenty-six) and 1909. More radically and more rapidly than any other European composer, Schoenberg moved from the mastery of late romantic symphonic chamber music embodied in the string sextet *Verklärte Nacht* to the post-tonal expressionism of the monodrama *Erwartung*. He did so by way of a remarkable succession of works in many different genres – a large-scale orchestral tone poem, two string quartets, a chamber symphony, a good number of songs and piano pieces. If that were not enough, he also made substantial progress with his largest completed work, *Gurrelieder*.

Music historians with a taste for dramatic generalisation can assert that, single-handedly, Schoenberg transformed music from something recognisably rooted in the familiar tonal traditions of Wagner and Brahms, Strauss and Mahler, into a kind of atonal expressionism that proclaimed the viability of truly new music at a time when the new century had barely begun. With its predominantly secular tone, Schoenberg's entire output over that decade might be thought of as essentially preliminary to the kind of struggles between the material and the metaphysical explored in later works such as *Die Jakobsleiter* and *Moses und Aron*, and preliminary also to the productive tensions between fixed and flexible moods and materials made possible by the development of the twelve-tone method after 1920. Yet the innovative eruptions specific to the decade 1899 to 1909 have had a profound influence over later compositional developments, to the present day: and, preliminary or not, at least some of the compositions from these years are more often heard, and more frequently discussed, than those from Schoenberg's later years.

Much of the most authoritative and substantial discussion of Schoenberg's rapid and radical evolution from post-Wagnerian romantic to post-tonal expressionist has appeared over the past ten to fifteen years, a time when many assumptions inherent in terms such as 'romantic' and 'expressionist', or 'tonal' and 'atonal', have been questioned as intensively as the music itself has been technically expounded. This handbook therefore has the opportunity to respond to these materials in ways which are accessible to a less academically specialised readership – not just those interested in Schoenberg, but those concerned with the whole nature of twentieth-century music's relation to the diverse stylistic traditions that preceded it. Much reference is made below to writings that offer far more extensive score quotation and far more elaborate technical explication than is possible, or perhaps desirable, in this handbook. Here the main objective is to place the compositions described in as wide-ranging and stimulating a collection of contexts as possible. More than a century on, Schoenberg's 'Night Music' retains its power to fascinate as well as to disturb, and those qualities gain in profile when some of the wider considerations of the 'Night Music' concept are brought forward into the light.

The Character of a Genre

'*Night Music* is cast in one large movement with four distinct sections. It inhabits a world of dreams, nightmares, moonlight, and darkness, beginning in a quasi-somnambulant state with a blurring of melodic lines and harmony.'[1] Writing about his fifteen-minute 2014 composition for cello and piano, the British composer Mark Simpson (b. 1988) continues with a descriptive account of musical moods and textures but no longer emphasises matters nocturnal. In this way, Simpson follows the common tendency to take a very basic initial aesthetic concept – Night Music – without then attempting to prescribe a set of characteristics so specific that they could not possibly be applied to any other aesthetic concept. Such a concept nevertheless becomes particularly significant for composers who use it frequently, in works of some substance. Two British composers, considerably more senior than Simpson, fit this label: Harrison Birtwistle (1934–2022), with his Dowland-haunted orchestral piece *The Shadow of Night* and Celan setting 'Tenebrae', and Brian

Ferneyhough (b. 1943) with the guitar pieces *Kurze Schatten II* and the opera *Shadowtime*. In such cases, the night-referring titles fit with a particular musical atmosphere that is much more pervasive in the composers' oeuvre than restriction to compositions whose titles directly reference nocturnal images would allow, an atmosphere that tends not to be found – or is only occasionally hinted at – in the music of composers with markedly different aesthetic and technical orientations.

An early work of Ferneyhough's – *Sonatas for String Quartet* (1967) – has an unusually restrained episode, with the marking 'notturnamente', which inspires a Schoenberg allusion from commentator Lois Fitch; it 'proceeds ... from a calm chordal passage into the closing polyphonic material of the section, in high register, marked "sereno e chiaro", the whole episode a transfigured night'.[2] Ferneyhough's music is a particularly interesting example in relation to this book's central subject – an aspect of Schoenberg's aesthetic that highlights a distinction between theological and materialist motives, and which makes a suitably tentative comparison between the thinking of the cultural philosopher Walter Benjamin (the subject of Ferneyhough's opera) and Schoenberg's compositional trajectory. There is a world of difference between the philosopher's way with such themes, as explored by the Benjamin commentator Graeme Gilloch,[3] and the composer's concern to use sound materials to animate ideas that might appear wholly materialist, wholly theological or to involve interplay between the two. That 'world of difference' requires a narrative that questions parallelisms as it explores them and dramatises the distinction between a central, ever-present subject, the composer, and a hovering, often submerged, context-provider, the philosopher. If this form of words puts the reader in mind of Thomas Mann's novel *Doctor Faustus*, and the tragicomedy of the exchanges between Schoenberg and Mann about its allusions to Schoenbergian twelve-tone technique, so much the better![4]

Prelude

Night and Nature

All days are nights to see till I see thee
And nights bright days when dreams do show thee me.

Shakespeare's Sonnet 43, of which these are the last two lines, is a
celebrated exercise in antithesis, as well as in the use of visible and
sounding similarities between words which embody difference –
'thee', 'me'. Writers on music are quick to point out that their
chosen subject matter is no less remarkable than English or any
other language in its ability to organise itself around patterns of
difference and similarity, and that such differences and similarities
can be aurally recognisable – a mental process of identification
comparable to that brought to bear by readers of poetry or prose.
Yet the fact remains that Shakespeare's art is based on materials –
words – which are no less relevant and useful to real life in the
everyday world. The meaning of terms such as 'night' and 'day' –
or their equivalents in other languages – is readily accessible to all
humans, but the musical materials used by any composer setting
Shakespeare's text (as Benjamin Britten did in his *Nocturne* of
1958) have no equivalent real-life meaning. As numerous publi-
cations attest, it is perfectly possible to describe in words what
those materials consist of, and to explain why the particular
musical combinations and characteristics chosen by Britten suit
Shakespeare's poem. But saying that 'the purely instrumental
Nocturne from Mendelssohn's *Midsummer Night's Dream*
music, like Britten's setting of Sonnet 43, can be categorised as
Night Music' is only to imply that the musical materials of both, as
pitches, rhythms and timbres, are capable of being characterised in
a manner appropriate to the title and association of things nocturnal. The same generic marker, as verbal definition, could be
applied to quite different musical materials, whether a nocturnal
text is present or not.

The connotations of 'night' are not confined to the hours of
complete darkness. Shakespeare's sonnet is not just about the
temporal divisions of night and day, sleeping and waking, but
about the associations between these events and a lover's per-
ceptions about himself and the one he loves. Other texts set by
Britten in *Nocturne* (the extract from Wordsworth's *The Prelude*,

4

particularly) explore different mental and physical states, where sleep is disturbed, and darkness as menace is the governing image, and it is through the common strands of content rather than the individual characteristics of each separate text that the collective label of 'Night Music' becomes viable. Compositions focusing on the nocturnal in this way might well be regarded as belonging to the even-wider category of Nature Music, acknowledging the common purpose of musical works that resist the lure of some kind of entirely abstract, 'purely musical' genre, such as fugue or canon. It is indeed the effect of experiencing the natural world at night, as distinct from experiencing particular emotions or events at night within an enclosed indoor space so that the 'night-ness' is essentially mental, that characterises many compositions which respond to texts or ideas of this kind, ranging in tone from the serene sublimity of Schumann's setting of Eichendorff's 'Mondnacht' to the nightmarish scenario unfolding in Schoenberg's setting of the Giraud/Hartleben poem 'Nacht' in *Pierrot lunaire*; and non-vocal compositions whose expressive characteristics (and titles) seem to have things in common with such settings might well attract the 'Night Music' label.

Pierrot lunaire will feature in some detail later in this text, but it is useful to mention one particular study of that work at this preliminary stage, one which does not directly describe it as Night Music but rather as 'Lunar Nexus'. In his article, Michael Cherlin argues that 'Schoenberg's early practice' emerges from a Romantic tradition where 'naturalistic images' were central, 'so it should come as no surprise that naturalistic tone-painting is fairly common in his music during the first decades of the twentieth century'. Cherlin instances '*Verklärte Nacht, Pelleas und Melisande, Gurre-Lieder, Das Buch der hängenden Gärten* and *Erwartung*' before noting that after World War I, with the emergence of the twelve-tone technique, 'naturalistic tone-painting seemed no longer to be part of Schoenberg's practice'.[5] What replaced it remains a matter of debate within Schoenberg studies, and a relatively recent indication of the challenges which arise when this issue is addressed in more than strictly compositional, technical terms can be found in a book by Matthew Arndt.[6] In essence, Arndt's thesis is that the 'musical thought' central to such works as *Verklärte Nacht* and *Erwartung*, in which 'naturalistic tone-painting' features prominently, has little need to engage with the aspects of spirituality that Arndt's title signals as salient. The real challenge therefore becomes to find ways of coherently conveying what those 'aspects of spirituality' involve.

The whole point of this book is to consider the nature of what I call Schoenberg's Night Music, not the music that displaced it, but it will still be useful to provide at least an outline of what that other Schoenberg was like. He had formally converted from Judaism to Protestantism at the age of twenty-three in 1898 and remained, officially, a Christian until July 1933, after more than a decade of experiencing the intensification of anti-Semitism in Europe that would drive him into American exile well before the outbreak of World War II. The association between religious faith and compositional concerns – between 'aspects of spirituality' on the one hand and thinking about issues connected to both traditional tonality and twelve-tone technique – is a topic many writers have explored, but a particularly specific interpretation is posited by Matthew Arndt in his claim that 'Schoenberg's return to Judaism coincides with his invention of twelve-tone composition in 1921–3 – and with his intense study of Schenker in 1922–3' (57).

For Arndt, something commonly represented in terms of complete opposition between Schoenberg, and a conservative music theorist, Heinrich Schenker (1868–1935), can look very different when what (in Arndt's view) Schoenberg and Schenker held 'spiritually' in common is brought into focus:

Schenker's and Schoenberg's conflict is a reflection of contradictions *within* their musical and spiritual ideas. They share a particular conception of the tone as an ideal sound realized in the spiritual eye of the genius. The tensions inherent in this largely psychological and material notion of the tone and this largely metaphysical notion of the genius shape both their musical *divergence* on the logical (technical) level of theory and composition, and their spiritual *convergence*, including their invention of the *Ursatz* and twelve-tone composition and their simultaneous return to Judaism. (3)

Arndt shares with other music theorists the perception that tonal music as Schenker defined it and non-tonal music as Schoenberg conceived it converged on the process of creating and then solving a problem: 'A piece of tonal music solves its problem by erasing all doubt about the ground tone, whereas a piece of non-tonal music solves its problem by erasing all trace of the ground tone as such'; Arndt then argues that 'Schoenberg's references to "renouncing the tonal centre" in his music are best understood as shorthand for "the negation of a tonal centre's *domination*"' (106–7), and it is erroneous to assume that 'renouncing the tonal centre' means literally abandoning or destroying tonality. In addition, Arndt sees these technical formulations as embodying an overriding ambition, which is to overcome the materiality of art, as Schoenberg arguably sought to do with some consistency from around 1912 onwards. Before that, and especially in his Night Music, Schoenberg had shown how beguiling or disturbing 'materiality' in music might be, resisting alienation to offer a measure of reconciliation with mundane reality.

Considerations of how Schoenberg's music might formulate and (in some cases) resolve technical problems arising from the changing character of his compositional style will feature later in this discussion. First, however, a few more preliminaries around the theme of words and music are in order. There are many reasons for writing about composers. A common strategy is to express admiration for the compositions themselves, and to try to convey what it is about their character and content that is admirable; the writer's appreciation seeks to gain the assent of other admirers, as well as to encourage and even convert more sceptical readers. For example, if I say that 'Beethoven's *Eroica* Symphony begins with unprecedented and unsurpassed exuberance and eloquence', this is a statement difficult to dispute on its own terms, despite being unqualified, simply because it is likely to be understood as enthusiastic opinion rather than the kind of clinically technical, analytical dissection that could withstand any amount of attempted counter-argument. Clearly, in avoiding specific details about harmonic progression or rhythmic organisation, my assertion about the *Eroica* implies but glides over the entire context of musical history from the beginning ('unprecedented') to the present day ('unsurpassed'). There may not have been an earlier symphonic movement that can be shown to provide an exact model for

Beethoven's, but it cannot be denied that in formal outline and this or that technical procedure, Beethoven was not literally creating something completely new. Similarly, while the euphoric sense of a fresh approach to a traditional genre, the symphony, might be vividly apparent every time one listens to the *Eroica*'s first movement, later examples from Mendelssohn's 'Italian' Symphony to Brahms's Symphony No. 3 and beyond can be claimed to equal, and even perhaps surpass, Beethoven's innovatory exuberance.

Of the favoured contexts for compositions seen by writers as admirable, matters of culture and philosophy loom large. That a composition emerges at a specific time and in a particular place locates it culturally, socially and historically, and that can bring any number of other social contexts to do with politics and/or religion, for example, not to mention gender and nationality, into play. But what of philosophy? As creative enterprises, writing music and writing philosophy might be regarded as parallel activities, conceiving an idea and presenting a working-out of its consequences. Yet to move from parallels to interactions, interpenetrations, is risky, at least if it is assumed that music can directly embody philosophical principles so naturally and completely that listeners informed of the connection and appreciative of what is involved will inevitably assent to the fusion of the two disciplines, composing and philosophising, provided it is understood that there is still a separation: the philosophy has come first (e.g. Nietzsche's *Also sprach Zarathustra*, written in 1883–5), and the composer, Richard Strauss (consciously or, conceivably, unconsciously) invents an appropriate musicalisation of philosophical ideas, or at least their expressive tone, in his tone poem with the same title (1895).

A concrete example is called for. In an important essay whose line of argument is fundamental to the present study and can be thought of as complementary in some respects to the work of Matthew Arndt, William E. Benjamin identifies a connection between Schoenberg's writings on music and Schopenhauer's idea that 'the composer reveals the inmost essence of the world and utters the most profound wisdom in a language which his reason does not understand'. But for a more evolved connection between Schoenberg's music and philosophy, Benjamin prefers

8

Nietzsche to Schopenhauer, at least for the short but crucial period between 1908 and 1911, when Schoenberg seemed closest to the Nietzschean idea of Dionysian ritual, where 'individuals merge in a paroxysm of annihilation, in which the pain of being destroyed recedes before the joy of becoming part of a higher creativity, that of the unitary life force'. As Benjamin reinforces the point, his own central idea is that 'Schoenberg's early atonal music instantiates Nietzsche's conception of Dionysian art – by reflecting a vision of life (nature) as essentially multiplex and conflicted'.[7] But, while listeners familiar with Nietzsche could well intuit some such connection without any knowledge of Schoenberg's own awareness or otherwise of any philosophical texts, listeners to *Erwartung* or Schoenberg's settings of Stefan George may hear the complexity and conflictedness without any necessary link to Nietzschean Dionysianism. The specific connection is a critical refinement born of breadth of knowledge and appreciation of the state of culture around 1909.

Aspects of these ideas will feature prominently in what follows, but for the moment it is useful to consider the very different interpretative context that arises when a different philosopher – one who actually wrote about Schoenberg – enters the frame. Whereas William Benjamin's essay makes much of what he describes as Schoenberg's 'shift from the emotional and necessarily private to the deliberate and communal' after 1912, Theodor Adorno's response to Schoenberg's overall development from late romanticism and 'free atonality' to the twelve-tone method can be defined in entirely musical terms. According to Alastair Williams, Adorno believed that although 'Beethoven marks the entry into modernity . . . it was not until the innovations of Schoenberg that the implications of Beethoven's artistic challenge were fully realized'. In strong contrast to Benjamin, who regards the religious impulse as central to Schoenberg's embrace of the 'unknowable' in his later twelve-tone music, Adorno retained Schoenberg's connection with 'the heart of Enlightenment rationality' as the composer struggled after 1920 'to invent a musical medium that would simultaneously enable more freedom and greater discipline'. 'Adorno put the dilemma as follows, still with music rather than some other

9

context in the centre: "the question that twelve-tone music directs the composer towards is not, how can musical meaning be organized, but rather: how can musical organization become meaningful?"[8] Whether that 'meaning' has to do primarily or even exclusively with a philosophy, a religion, a political tendency or simply an aesthetic intuition seems to be a secondary matter.

As it happens, one of Adorno's earlier essays (1929) has the title 'Night Music' (*Nachtmusik*), though the reader will not find the concept or its significance spelt out in Adorno's actual text.[9] It is therefore a provocation to speculate both on that title and also on Adorno's dedication of the essay to his own teacher Alban Berg, in the year when Berg was beginning concentrated work on his second opera *Lulu*. The brief indication of different aspects of musical meaning that come into focus when either Nietzsche (as read by Benjamin) or Adorno (as read by Williams) provides the context underlines the inevitable tension between compositions as 'notes on paper' or 'sounds as sounds', and compositions as signifying entities whose titles, texts and contexts suggest interpretative associations which can vary enormously from critic to critic. My own choice of 'Night Music' as a consistent point of reference suggests concreteness rather than abstraction, an emphasis on the material to cloud if not entirely exclude the metaphysical, and on the physical and psychological specifics of periods of time known to the whole of humanity as the marked opposite of day. With the broad evolutionary context of music history in mind, and particularly the differences between expressionistic early modernism and the romanticism that preceded it, Night Music after 1900 is distinct from earlier Night Music. Even if one has some sympathy with those like Christopher Hailey who have downplayed the relevance of expressionism to music, as 'more descriptive convenience than historical reportage, an evocation of a syntax that is distorted, violent, or emotionally tortured', something 'vague' enough to be applied to both Charles Ives and Gesualdo[10] as well as Schoenberg and Webern around the years 1908–13 is also distinctive enough to be differentiated from other varieties of emotional intensity and formal instability. The expressionist sense of night as a time of fear, unease, even of haunting by spectres, fits with what William Benjamin seems to have had in mind in claiming that 'the unprecedented leaps Schoenberg made' in his music between 1908 and 1909 'arose from and were probably made possible by an essentially antirational view of art';[11] and if there is a genuine connection between Night Music and the 'antirational' in a non-religious sense, it might be expected that spirituality as perhaps supra-rational would displace Night Music by something altogether more rational in an attempt to change the emphasis to a music – eventually twelve-tone – which Benjamin describes as 'more deliberate and communal' in ethos (1).

This short book appears in the wake of some of the most ambitious and wide-ranging work on Schoenberg ever undertaken, and its concerns could easily appear modest and parochial in comparison. As well as Benjamin's characterisation of a career-length trajectory in terms of 'religious thought', and the initiatives of Jack Boss and Matthew Arndt in demonstrating the musical idea's pervasive relation to both tonality and atonality, including twelve-tone music, there is Julie Brown's argument that Schoenberg 'was one of many artists and intellectuals committed to a Wagnerian ideology of cultural regeneration, ideology which had been given a contemporary idealist – indeed, intellectually radical – spin by his Viennese contemporary Otto Weininger', and in which the 'renunciation of tonality' was a moral, ethical move, 'an essential step in the liberation of music from the domination of tonality'.[12] Brown reinforces the cultural as well as ideological aspects of Schoenberg's thought when she claims that 'a coherent explanation for Schoenberg's various creative and theoretical innovations, as well as his responses to the changing politics in Germany, emerges when one reads certain key artistic moves alongside Wagner's theories concerning the "Jew's" position in German culture' (6). At the same time, Brown admits that 'when it comes to talking about music's social meanings we must ... acknowledge that musical hermeneutics are intrinsically hazardous and can never exhaust art's dialogically self-renewing cultural meanings' (7). So even when the field of discourse is narrowed down to matters of music's apparently direct response to the time of day or night, and human behaviour within that particular environment, we do well to recall Schoenberg's apprehension that it was music's nature to be 'felt' rather than 'known', or 'known' through being 'felt'.

If Brown is right to highlight 'his desire to gain direct access to the idealized metaphysical realm' (14), then the musical and musico-dramatic consequences of that desire serve to distance Schoenberg after 1913 from much of what was involved in his earlier music, when progress from embracing to renouncing tonality, as traditionally understood, was in play. If 'the idealized metaphysical realm' is the goal, the materialist basis of modernism is called into question, and Night Music's resistance to embracing the ineffable will be challenged as never before. I will therefore explore the degree to which an account of Schoenberg's Night Music is also an account of his earlier music – music whose omissions are provocative and, it would appear, embodied evolutionary forces that shaped Schoenberg's challenging career as would-be cultural regenerator.

Schoenberg and Night Music

As a composer and teacher who owed more to self-instruction and advice from friends than to formal university or conservatoire music courses, Schoenberg never lost his immense respect for the genres and textures of the great German 'Bach to Brahms' inheritance. His concern that all students of composition should master traditional techniques of tonal harmony and counterpoint underpinned his extensive writings about music and explains his conviction that contemporary post-tonal techniques, including the twelve-tone method, should not be taught; real composers, as distinct from students, must find their own way, their own individual voice. But Schoenberg also had the greatest respect for the music of Liszt, Wagner, Mahler and Strauss. Accordingly, he was never likely to share the conviction, most explicit among his contemporaries in the theorist Heinrich Schenker, that texted and any kind of frankly illustrative music risked debasing the essential purity of a mode of expression that referred primarily to its own purely musical materials and processes, and not to the analogies with verbal concepts and literary structures that talking and writing about even the most apparently abstract forms of music made unavoidable.

In his early compositions of the 1890s, while fully conformant with the inherited principles of the enriched tonal system then favoured by Mahler, Strauss and Zemlinsky, Schoenberg began to reveal a willingness to rethink the scope and character of long-established compositional genres. So, although by 1899 he had worked on songs, piano pieces and string quartets, his decision to compose *Verklärte Nacht* – a string sextet whose title, form and content stemmed from a poem – seems like a consciously nonconformist gesture. By 1900, there was, of course, an abundance of purely orchestral compositions with poetic or dramatic sources, but throughout the nineteenth century, chamber music had remained essentially abstract, on a par with sonatas and symphonies rather than with tone poems. Perhaps because of their origins in the single movements of instrumental dance suites, there were many genres of solo piano music that had poetic or pictorial connections, as well as great numbers of piano transcriptions (often of vocal works) that featured prominently in recital programmes. But chamber compositions for between two and nine players had tended only to admit a degree of cross-generic identity when, as most familiarly with Schubert's 'Trout' Quintet, an existing song was used as the theme for a set of variations. It would therefore be understandable if, by the end of the nineteenth century, the feeling should emerge (as part of that restless, relatively radical impulse eventually designated modernism) that chamber-music genres were ripe for the kind of formal transformation that poetic, potentially vocal associations could provide. If the argument was ever put forward that chamber groups inevitably lacked the colouristic range and resonance that orchestras could bring to symphonic poems, it would be part of the modernist spirit to discount such an argument – and especially when the essence of the poetic source was not something expansively exotic but essentially intimate, like a pair of lovers placed in a nocturnal setting that emphasised local details as well as more distant vistas.

As a title or generic indicator, Night Music after 1900 is primarily a phenomenon of the ongoing modernist era, when it has been rare to find compositions with the sublime naivety of Haydn's emphatic switch in *The Creation* from darkness 'on the face of the deep' (chromatic C minor) to the response – 'and there was light' – to God's peremptory instruction 'Let there be light!' (diatonic C major). Modernism's special unease with sentimental notions of the cosiness of the 'Holy Night' of Christ's birth was mocked in Alfred Schnittke's *Stille Nacht* for violin and piano (1978), and its intentionally crude distortions of the well-known carol seem like a knowing sneer at the twentieth century's liking for musical representations of darkness and despair, something Karlheinz Stockhausen also sought to counter in his monumental, highly idiosyncratic and anti-materialist seven-opera cycle *Licht* (also begun in 1978). But Night Music was nowhere acknowledged by Schoenberg to be an independent genre. 'Night Music' or 'Night Piece' as titles may indeed be found after 1900 as alternatives to the more romantic Nocturne or Notturno; but Schoenberg would probably have thought of such titles as generically cognate with the Serenade (as in Mozart's *Serenata Notturna* and *Eine kleine Nachtmusik*) as well as with the 'so-called "Free Forms"', including rhapsodies and preludes, which he instances in *Structural Functions of Harmony*.[13] Such a category would clearly suit one of his own apprentice efforts – a *Notturno* from 1896 for solo violin, strings and harp (called 'Adagio' in the surviving manuscript) – and all such categories were capable of putting into practice his concept of the 'Musical Idea' not simply as a basic theme or melodic shape, but as a tripartite formal framework progressing from the presentation of a technical problem and the elaboration of the materials presented to illustrate the problem to an eventual solution or resolution. That such a formal notion gave rise to inherent expressive qualities to do with tension, conflict, ambiguity and then to some kind of closure or fulfilment undoubtedly enhanced the usefulness of this formulation of the Musical Idea as a source of compositions which were not thought of as essentially or entirely abstract.[14]

Serenades might be either single movements or suite-like collections of dances and other miniature forms, and there is enough consistency around the idea of formal dances as being mainly evening events, and serenades being performed after dark in the street below the window of a lover's bedroom (as in Act 1 of *Don Giovanni* or Act 2 of *Die Meistersinger*), to legitimise the generic link between 'Serenade' and 'Night Music'. Mozart's four-movement *Eine kleine Nachtmusik* might be more Sinfonietta than Dance Suite, but it fits the sense of incidental music for a social event taking place in the evening like a ball or banquet. In the romantic era, the newly acquired prominence of the intimate keyboard Nocturne pioneered by John Field and perfected by Chopin shifted the associations of Night Music away from the collectively social to the separate status of fated lovers facing separation when, in opera, night was the obvious time for an assignation which might be lyrically serene (Berlioz's Dido and Aeneas in *Les Troyens*), ecstatically declamatory (Wagner's *Tristan and Isolde*) or even expressionistically deranged, as in Schoenberg's own *Erwartung*. As for 'Nachtmusik' as a title, its most striking use in an instrumental work came a few years after *Verkärte Nacht*, when Mahler used it for the second and fourth movements of his Seventh Symphony (1904–5), the first 'one of Mahler's most fantastic inspirations ... with sinister military march elements', the second 'an intimate pastoral serenade'.[15]

Wagner, hugely influential on composers of Mahler's and Schoenberg's generations, not only used the unprecedented length of his central dialogue scene for Tristan and Isolde to traverse a vast gamut of emotional states but also provided a text in which bright daylight and Stygian darkness were set in opposition as creating impossible and ideal contexts in which humans might discover and enact the truth about themselves. Though Wagner's stage directions at the start of Act 2 of *Tristan* specify a summer night's beguiling ('Anmutige') garden setting, implying an actively benign and stable social context, for the obsessed lovers the location reinforces the appeal of an abstracted state in which a kind of delirium can be shared, so intensely that the sharers believe themselves to be fused into a single super-real identity. Here Wagner's Night Music depicts the drama's central and most crucial action, culminating in the exposure of the lovers that leads in turn to their separation and shared deaths as they fail to rediscover that 'magical realm of night' which was their only hope of a fulfilled, shared life. In this sense, Wagner's drama charts the discovery and loss of Night Music as ideal and essence. It makes its effect through transcending an entirely nocturnal cast of mind, and it follows that to think of a composition as Night Music is to retreat from the kind of vastly complex social and spiritual ambitions that characterise Wagner's major compositions. Yet even on a smaller scale like that of *Verklärte Nacht*, where Night Music is the entirety of a work that traces the hopes and fears of impassioned lovers, there can still be considerable contrast between serene and uneasy situations. An untexted piece of Night Music can hardly let the daylight in without irreparably compromising the genre. Thirteen years would elapse after *Verklärte Nacht* before Schoenberg gave a texted composition ('Nacht' in *Pierrot lunaire*) this specific title – years in which his most intense and extensive workings with the genre would take place.

Notes

1. Mark Simpson, liner notes with NMC D225 (2016), 1.
2. Lois Fitch, *Brian Ferneyhough* (Bristol: Intellect, 2013), 162.
3. Graeme Gilloch, *Walter Benjamin: Critical Constellations* (Cambridge: Polity Press, 2002).
4. See *The Doctor Faustus Dossier*, ed. E. Randol Schoenberg (Berkeley: University of California Press, 2018).
5. Michael Cherlin, '*Pierrot lunaire* as Lunar Nexus', *Music Analysis* 31/2 (July 2012): 176–215 (176, 211).
6. Matthew Arndt, *The Musical Thought and Spiritual Lives of Heinrich Schenker and Arnold Schoenberg* (London: Routledge, 2018). Page references in text.
7. William E. Benjamin, 'Abstract Polyphonies: The Music of Schoenberg's Nietzschean Moment', in *Political and Religious Ideas in the Works of Arnold Schoenberg*, ed. Charlotte M. Cross and Russell A. Berman (New York: Garland, 2000), 1–39. Page references in text.
8. Alastair Williams, *New Music and the Claims of Modernity* (Aldershot: Ashgate, 1997), p. 32. Williams cites the translation of Adorno's *Philosophy of Modern Music* by Anne Mitchell and Wesley Blomster (1973). For a slightly different version, see *Philosophy of New Music*, trans. Robert Hullot-Kentor (Minneapolis: University of Minnesota Press, 2006), 54.
9. T. W. Adorno, *Night Music: Essays on Music, 1920–1962*, ed. Rolf Tiedemann, trans. Wieland Hoban (Calcutta: Seagull Books, 2009), 81–93.
10. Christopher Hailey, 'Musical Expressionism: The Search for Autonomy', in *Expressionism Reassessed*, ed. Shulamith Behr,

David Fanning and Douglas Jarman (Manchester: Manchester University Press, 1993), 103–111 (104).

11. Benjamin, 'Abstract Polyphonies', 2.
12. Julie Brown, *Schoenberg and Redemption* (Cambridge: Cambridge University Press, 2014), 2. Further page references in text.
13. Arnold Schoenberg, *Structural Functions of Harmony*, 2nd ed., ed. Leonard Stein (New York: Norton, 1969), 165–91.
14. Schoenberg's own writings on this topic are published in *The Musical Idea and the Logic, Technique, and Art of its Presentation*, ed. and trans. Patricia Carpenter and Severine Neff (New York: Columbia University Press, 1995). For extensive theoretical and analytical development of the subject, see Jack Boss, *Schoenberg's Twelve-Tone Method: Symmetry and the Musical Idea* (Cambridge: Cambridge University Press, 2014).
15. Deryck Cooke, *Guide to Mahler's Symphonies* (London: BBC, 1960), 37.

2

VERKLÄRTE NACHT

Background

The string sextet *Verklärte Nacht* (drafted during the summer of
1899, just before his twenty-fifth birthday) is not only
Schoenberg's first large-scale piece of Night Music, but his first
distinctively personal large-scale composition, the first work
which, with hindsight, radiates a potential for high-level accom-
plishment all the more remarkable in a composer who had not
been conventionally trained in a major Viennese institution.
Nevertheless, from the age of eleven or so, Schoenberg had the
invaluable experience of contact with Oskar Adler (1875–1955).
Adler, who taught him the basics of music theory and also
encouraged Schoenberg to play chamber music as violinist and
cellist, became a medical doctor with wide interests in science
and philosophy; Schoenberg was still writing to him in the last
few months of his life, by which time Adler was living in
London, Schoenberg having failed to arrange a proposed move
from Vienna to California for him in the 1930s.

Between the ages of seventeen and twenty-one, Schoenberg
worked in a bank, but his friendships with Adler and other musically minded contemporaries, especially the composer and conductor Alexander von Zemlinsky (1872–1942), only two years
his senior, encouraged him to risk embarking on a hand-to-
mouth freelance career as a choral conductor while also working
on orchestrations and vocal scores of operettas and other compositions for the Viennese music publishers Universal Edition. This
range of practical experience and activity came at a time when
Mahler and Strauss were the most prominent of younger composers, and literature and the visual arts in Vienna provided vital

stimulus to innovative aesthetic ideas in the final years of a century that had begun with the supreme musical achievements – all in or near Vienna – of Haydn, Mozart, Beethoven and Schubert. It set the scene for Schoenberg's remarkable blend of deep respect for tradition and equally deep desire to find radically new ways of expressing that respect in musical forms that responded even more forensically than in Mahler or Strauss to the different challenges thrown down by the instrumental music of Brahms and the vocal music of Wagner.

Schoenberg's own early efforts included a large number of songs, and his setting of Richard Dehmel's poem 'Warnung', dating from May 1899, a few months before *Verklärte Nacht*, was used by one of Schoenberg's leading biographers, H. H. Stuckenschmidt, to demonstrate the composer's early attainment of a 'synthesis' in which 'the chromaticism of *Tristan* is married to the symphonic procedure which Brahms had brought into the field of song'.[1] In a definitive account of all of Schoenberg's Dehmel settings, Walter Frisch documented salient aspects of the affinity between poet and composer.[2] This rich mixture of competing and complementary musical qualities played its part in fuelling Schoenberg's advance into the creative maturity and sophistication of the large-scale single-movement sextet, which offers a further blend of competing qualities in its fusion of naturalistically pictorial tone poem and abstract chamber music, moving decisively beyond the non-pictorial symphonism of Brahms's early pair of string sextets (1858–65). It might also embody a young composer's implied reservations about the orchestral tone poems of that decade's leading exponent, Richard Strauss. *Don Juan*, *Tod und Verklärung*, *Till Eulenspiegel*, *Also sprach Zarathustra* and *Ein Heldenleben* had all been composed between 1888 and 1898, yet as Bojan Bujić has pointed out, the most direct allusion to Straussian qualities in *Verklärte Nacht* comes in the similarity between its opening 'trudging' motif and a theme in Strauss's early Symphony in F minor (1883–4); and while both composers use exaltedly restrained and richly sonorous major chords to mark their transfiguratory apotheoses, the difference in weight between Strauss's full orchestra in *Tod und Verklärung* and Schoenberg's chamber group keeps closer affinities at bay. None of Schoenberg's own ideas for orchestral tone poems progressed very far before his work on *Pelleas und Melisande* in 1902.[3]

In 1912, Schoenberg wrote to Dehmel in a tone of retrospective appreciation: 'your poems have had a decisive influence on my musical development. It was because of them that I was for the first time compelled to seek a new tone in lyric writing. That is, I found it without having to look, by reflecting in music what your poems stirred up in me.' 'Reflecting in music' seems to allow for a connection that goes beyond, or even bypasses, setting the actual words, and Dehmel himself, with his argument that poetry was above all 'a rhythmic work of art', and that music can raise us from 'confusion of feeling' into 'that magic circle of purely rhythmic forces that has transformed the excited mind of the poet into artistically anticipating tension', appears to have sensed the appeal of musical responses to poetry that were not simply settings of the words.[4]

The poems by Dehmel that Schoenberg set two years before *Verklärte Nacht*, in September 1897, were in the tradition of Heine's nature-reflecting love lyrics – poetry celebrated in the settings by Schubert and Schumann which Schoenberg would have known well. When it came to Dehmel's 1896 collection *Weib und Welt*, which included 'Verklärte Nacht', Vilain suggests that the three poems Schoenberg set earlier in 1899 strain 'emotions to their limits, while both ironizing and refining them' (15); the more complex and subtle the poems themselves became, the more the composer may have sensed the impossibility of matching those particular verbal and poetic qualities in his own medium. The answer, when it came to 'Verklärte Nacht', was therefore not to set the actual text but rather to *reflect* what the poem 'stirred up' in him as he contemplated its character and content; the task of actually setting that text was taken up by Oskar Fried (1871– 1941), who composed a rather Straussian scena for soprano, tenor and piano, later orchestrated, in 1901.

With the text implied but not set, it is difficult to associate Schoenberg's sextet precisely with any kind of 'new lyric tone' within the prevailing style of concerted chamber music, although the generic contrast between the sextet and the non-programmatic

String Quartet in D major he had completed two years earlier (not published until the 1960s) certainly broke new ground in the intensity of the visual imagery in relation to Dehmel's poem that the music conjures up. Yet it was in small-scale song composition rather than larger-scale instrumental music that Schoenberg would advance most decisively towards a more complex and expressionistic style over the decade after 1899: that style did not become prominent in his instrumental and orchestral music until the String Quartet No. 2 and Five Orchestral Pieces of 1907–9, and in *Verklärte Nacht* it is romantic intensity rather than expressionistic turbulence that is uppermost.

There appears to be a more direct connection between the erotic fervour of this music, as well as in the three Dehmel settings made around the same time, and Schoenberg's relationship with Mathilde von Zemlinsky (begun in 1899 during their summer idyll in Payerbach) than with any academic considerations about how best to attempt a decisive departure from the kind of chamber music conventions he had very effectively deployed before. By the same token, *Verklärte Nacht* sounds more Wagnerian than Brahmsian. There are particularly direct associations with the 'ew'ge Nacht, süsse Nacht' of *Tristan* Act 2 in the sextet's portrayal of Dehmel's 'hohe, helle Nacht', which fixes the nocturnal setting as relatively benign, with no sign of impending storms. The progression from initial anxiety and apprehension to ecstatic certainty is also common to both, though there is no hint in either Dehmel or Schoenberg of the Wagnerian aftermath – that such 'certainty' is a delusion; that while night appears to be the time of serenity and security, day can only be a time of disorientation and despair. Of course, Wagner's music drama eventually concludes with Isolde's ecstatic vision of her eternal union in death with Tristan, a state that takes the drama well beyond the kind of local, domestic circumstances that seem to apply for Dehmel's lovers, and likewise for the human persona represented in Strauss's *Tod und Verklärung* (1888–9).

The notion of 'transfiguration' projected in *Verklärte Nacht* is quite different from Isolde's solitary apotheosis and might even be associated, given the triumphantly dominant masculinity in Dehmel's text, with the no less serene (though also more solemn)

Example 2.1 Schoenberg, *Verklärte Nacht* Op. 4, bars 224–9

ending of Strauss's tone poem *Ein Heldenleben* (first performed in Frankfurt in March 1899). As the following discussion will show, however, Schoenberg's response to Wagner's music in his sextet might be more fruitfully heard in relation to his reflection on what Wagner himself had come to regard as the polarised pillars of his new kind of dramatic structure: on the one hand, 'the art of transition' sought to sustain the listener's attention by effecting gradual connections between separate stages of the structure, while on the other hand, what Wagner called 'rhetorical dialectics'[5] could embody moments of disjunction and divergence where the whole point was the shock of disconnection. At their most basic, such moments could involve the use of a pair of unrelated chords placed either side of a sudden silence. For example, in *Verklärte Nacht* it is tempting to regard the unadorned harmonic shift from E flat minor to D major at the work's centre-point (Example 2.1, bars 224–9) as a startling, momentarily disorientating effect, despite the fact that the chords actually share one pitch – G flat/F sharp. In abstract form, this material prefigures the post-tonal major/minor trichord – D, E flat, G flat/F sharp – that is so prominent in *Pierrot*'s nightmarish 'Nacht'.

Form as Narrative

The connection between the five-part form of Dehmel's poem and that of *Verklärte Nacht* is arguably more explicit than is provided for in the kind of transformed symphonic or sonata form-plan favoured by several commentators. Dehmel's poem is structured almost as a brief dramatic script, with three different voices involved – a narrator, whose three scene-setting sections frame statements by first the woman, then the man. The narrations even have a touch of the stage direction about them, the first ending 'the voice of the woman speaks', the second 'the voice of the man speaks'. The rhythms of the first stanza suggest the moderate, trudging pace of walkers who are preoccupied, more concerned with choosing the right moment to talk than with getting to a destination. The setting seems to be autumnal, even wintry, the trees leafless, the air chilly: but there is also bright moonlight, without the shadows caused by passing clouds. When the woman speaks, she tells her lover – her husband? – that she is guilty of an impulsive encounter at a moment when she was 'longing for the cares and joys of motherhood', and so, we infer, became pregnant from a brief, loveless liaison. Now, however, 'life has taken its revenge' – so it is as if she expects her present companion to reject her, and in the second short passage of narration her expression is described as troubled, her anxious face exposed by the moonlight. But in his response, the man immediately seeks to put her mind at rest. He contrasts the 'cold sea' they inhabit – presumably in terms of how their families and friends will think of them – with the warmth he feels for her, in harmony with the glistening aura of the moonlight, and in a strangely complex image he speculates that the woman will return his warm feelings as if he were also a child of hers. The final passage of narration then describes how they embrace before walking on through the still, bright night (Dehmel's words – 'hohe, helle' – hint at a kind of elevated, even holy emotional state, the initial apprehension transformed into hope and joy).

Verklärte Nacht's primary generic identity as a single-movement tone poem rather than a multi-movement string sextet after the Brahmsian model has naturally led to discussions that place it in the tradition of such orchestral compositions by Liszt and Strauss, and had Schoenberg succeeded in completing the symphonic poem *Frühlings Tod*, which he had considered writing slightly earlier in 1898, it would doubtless have reinforced such provenance, inspired as that was by a poem by Nikolas Lenau, whose 'Schilflied' Schoenberg had set back in 1893. However, those precursors tended to be based around 'classic' rather than contemporary texts – Liszt's *Hamlet*, Strauss's *Macbeth* – and certainly not (at least before Strauss's *Symphonia Domestica* of

1902–3) to reference up-to-date domestic dramas of the kind that Dehmel was writing about. Evocative landscapes, legendary and/ or heroic historical events were other favoured sources; but Dehmel's poem reads more like the outline of a drama that turns convention on its head by showing how a 'fallen' woman is redeemed by the love of a good man. There are few if any parallels with a romantic tragedy like Verdi's *La Traviata* (1852–3), deriving from a Dumas play in which an essentially decadent social circumstance is ennobled by highlighting human qualities of honesty and selflessness, and in which masculine stuffiness is shamed by female physical vulnerability and spiritual strength. Rather, Dehmel's synopsis seems closer to *Jenůfa*, the veristic operatic drama by Janáček (1894–7, 1901–4), in which the heroine, recovering from the trauma of her illegitimate child's drowning by her stepmother, finds new purpose and contentment (and the ability to forgive the stepmother) with her understanding lover. When he came to plan for his own first opera in 1908, Schoenberg would choose a very different scenario from the ultimately upbeat narrative of *Jenůfa* or *Verklärte Nacht*; as a 'monodrama', *Erwartung* would have no place for the masculine voice, and its text is not so much redolent of decadence as of doubt. But neither the distraught wife nor the dead husband in *Erwartung* were heroic figures, and the monodrama's single-movement structure ultimately dissolves its own consistent uncertainties as decisively as *Verklärte Nacht*'s serene and stable ending resolves that drama's initial uneasiness.

Walter Frisch, whose analytical study of the sextet and its sources remains the definitive account of all its aspects, declares that Schoenberg's 'remarkable development' in 1899, culminating in the sextet, 'grew directly out of his search for a musical language appropriate to the poetry of [Dehmel's] *Weib und Welt*'.[6] In particular, his work on the song 'Erwartung' in August 1899, just before the sextet was begun, involved a poem about 'a nocturnal encounter between a pair of lovers', and 'both are framed by stanzas in which a narrator describes the scene ... a feature that inspired Schoenberg to create in both works a broad recapitulatory closing section' (98). Probably in 1898, or early in 1899, he had begun a different tone poem for string sextet, *Totes Winkel*, based

on a poem by Gustav Falke, but this seems to have been abandoned after thirty-four bars, perhaps because Schoenberg decided
that Dehmel's poem would be a more appropriate choice for
a work in that medium. Frisch surveys the evidence in support of
his claim that 'the sextet was conceived and written during
a relatively short span in September 1899, then revised intermit-
tently over the course of the fall, so that the complete score was
finished on 1 December' (110). This was the time of Schoenberg's
closest association with Zemlinsky. Back in 1896, Zemlinsky had
conducted an earlier night-piece of Schoenberg's, the *Notturno* for
solo violin, strings and harp, along with his own Eichendorff
setting *Waldgespräch*. It has also been suggested that Zemlinsky
himself had begun to compose a setting of Dehmel's 'Die Magd'
for soprano and string sextet only to abandon it around the time
that Schoenberg conceived the idea of a *Verklärte Nacht* sextet;
whether there is a significant connection between these two events
is not clear.[7]

In his overview of the sextet's formal design, Frisch takes note
of the disparate views of other commentators – Webern's 'free
fantasy' at one extreme, a single-movement sonata form at the
other. Frisch tends more in the Webern direction, with the claim
that the work is 'shaped by thematic and large-scale harmonic
processes lying largely outside the sonata tradition'.[8] This formula
provides an initial sense of the importance Frisch attaches to
connections and continuities: being shaped by processes that lie
'outside the sonata tradition' does not mean that the music is
loosely or randomly assembled from disparate segments, as
a continuous sequence of separate miniatures. But Frisch is no
less persuaded that 'while some of these compositional procedures
can be seen clearly to relate to traditional instrumental forms, the
actual thematic-formal structure of both parts of *Verklärte Nacht* is
sui generis' (122). Of particular importance in this respect is
exploring 'the possible intersections between what might be called
diatonic/dominant and chromatic/half-step worlds'; and in using
the crucial concept of 'intersection', Frisch leaves open the possibility that the hierarchic 'diatonic/dominant' world of traditional
tonal organisation and the symmetrical 'chromatic/half-step'
world of what Schoenberg would eventually term 'extended

tonality'[9] might constructively coexist in an equilibrium of alternatives, allowing that dramatic disparity could be just as positive and necessary a formal feature in this work as smooth transition and transformation. In these terms, what is 'sui generis' is the kind of early modernism, balancing centripetal against centrifugal forces, found in Wagner's music dramas and briefly discussed by Wagner himself in 'On the application of music to the drama'.

Verklärte Nacht in Detail

Jack Boss's projected three-volume study of Schoenberg's music will provide the most detailed demonstration of how a 'Musical Idea' can underpin works as apparently disparate as *Verklärte Nacht*, *Erwartung* and the Op. 33a Piano Piece. *Verklärte Nacht* is the first work in which this problem-defining-and-solving process appears as a fully mature and relevant concept, while also being sufficiently consistent in its traditional tonal grammar to lend itself to layered voice-leading analysis along Schenkerian lines.[10] At the very beginning, Schoenberg allows gradually intensifying chromatic inflections of the initial melodic minor D tonality (with C natural present only as a passing melodic tone) to transform the expressive character of the music from something rather sober and reticent into a much more frankly emotional and gesturally explicit language (see the second cello and second viola lines in the bars before Figure B). Then, a new turning motif (very Wagnerian in tone) appears at Figure B itself (Example 2.2, bars 21–6), and feverish tremolandi and rapid arpeggios quickly lead to the section, marked 'somewhat faster' (bar 29), that begins the woman's confession. While there is quite a strong change of texture and spacing at bar 22, and a clear local shift away from diatonic D minor triads to more dissonant sevenths, the basic harmonic continuity is enriched rather than fractured, and there is a sufficiently consistent anchoring of a bass line moving from D to G to A in the first stanza music (bars 1–28) to suggest an overall background progression for the section. But, as is often the case in nineteenth-century romantic music, chromaticism and relatively mild dissonance soon create a sense of anxiety and agitation, and this more unstable tone will predominate during

26

Example 2.2 Schoenberg, *Verklärte Nacht* Op. 4, bars 21–6

the Stanza 2 section, as the woman's explanation of her predica-
ment unfolds.

At quite an early stage (from bar 29), her agitation explodes and
collapses into hesitancy – an instance of the importance of rhythmic characterisation, matching Dehmel's view of the significance

Example 2.3 Schoenberg, *Verklärte Nacht* Op. 4, bars 41–5

of rhythmic patterning in poetry (see again note 4); and this moment (bar 42) is where Schoenberg introduces that 'single uncatalogued dissonance' that so rattled the critical dovecotes in conservative Vienna at its first performance (Example 2.3, bars 41–5). As is often pointed out, this chord (bar 42) is approached (across one beat's silence) by step in each part from a D minor dominant seventh. But the strength of the successive dissonances, especially that played with a strong accent on the first beat of bar 43, is less an enrichment of a unifying tonality than a rhetorical suspension or even demolition, however temporary, of that tonality, the first time in *Verklärte Nacht* that an unequivocal darkness of spirit emerges, even if the moon continues to shine.

Reducing this chordal passage (bars 41–5) to a simple diatonic progression in D minor – tonic 6/4, dominant 5/3 – might be justified to the extent that practised listeners could retain a sense of D's sustained tonic status extending across the whole of the Stanza 1 music into the early stages of Stanza 2. But from now on the single-flat key signature is less and less relevant as a prime controller of tonal identity, even before the signature actually changes to four sharps at bar 100. The brusque replacement of a possible tonic chord in bar 46 by a diminished seventh initiates a four-bar segment whose insistent motivic content (a semitone within a tritone deriving from the first violin motive in bars 43–4) freezes into an indefinite harmonic space whose open-endedness is enhanced by the general pause at the end of bar 49. A continuously evolving thematic process restarts in bar 50, and commentators keen on literal parallelisms between music and poetic situation might argue that the shift in the main thematic line from first cello to first violin at bar 55 (Example 2.4) implies dialogue between the

Example 2.4 Schoenberg, *Verklärte Nacht* Op. 4, bars 50–5

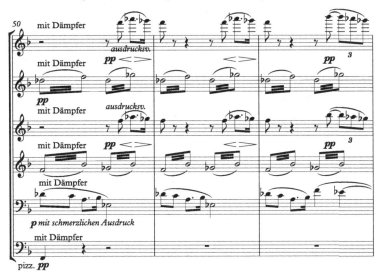

lovers, not just the female monologue that is the poem's second stanza. Nevertheless, it should be obvious that the intricate poly-phonic fabric of Schoenberg's music cannot simply be texturally mapped onto the pair of monologues that comprise the bulk of the poem. If anything, it must be the 'unspoken' interaction of sympathy and concern between the lovers while just one of them is actually speaking that the music 'literally' represents. After all, the printing of the poem in the score just before the first page of music can have a double function: as an indication of the inevitable disparities between the two media, but also as a declaration of close and consistent parallelism between the two.

There is an unmistakable process of intensification in connection with the lovers' mutual engagement as the tempo quickens progressively and the motivic repetitions grow increasingly insistent. When the process of repetition reaches its elemental one-beat minimum, or liquidation, in bar 99, the harmony attains a quality of maximum brightness with the second inversion E major chord: here, with the change of signature, the marking 'dolce' and the move from dominant preparation to inflected tonic at bar 105, Schoenberg surely had in mind the specific moment of the woman's concern for and commitment to her unborn child, mentioned straightaway in the poem but perhaps held in reserve by the composer to suit the expressive profile of this supremely volatile Stanza 2 episode. The effusive warmth of the E major music soon passes, however, and an even more disturbed spirit emerges ('etwas unruhiger'). From bar 124 to 175, the music is closest to the kind of 'free fantasy' chosen by Webern in his description of the work as a whole, where the alternation of brief recitative-like and cadenza-like outbursts suggests a generic profile in flux between opera and concerto. A moment of maximum textural breakdown and tonal occlusion occurs at bar 132 (Example 2.5, bars 131–4) as Schoenberg embarks on a passage of well-nigh melodramatic fervour, straining his chosen medium to its utmost (his arrangement of the work for string orchestra actually reduces the tensions of such textures, given the well-upholstered fullness of tone provided by a much larger ensemble, including double basses). This mood of maximum tension nevertheless serves a vital structural purpose, as a climax is reached with the forceful and suddenly much slower return of the form-dividing cadential progression from bars 41–45, here with a much richer textural layout and a different harmonic continuation which breaks off inconclusively (bar 187). The passage which follows functions

Example 2.5 Schoenberg, *Verklärte Nacht* Op. 4, bars 131–4

musically as a transition to Stanza 3 (clearly recalling Stanza 1's trudging gait), and vividly implying a stern masculine attempt to calm the situation after the well-nigh hysterical flights of the preceding episode.

The emphatic, bell-like accents of Stanza 3 support a texture that fits a B flat melodic minor tonality, and although the pure tonic triad itself is absent, this harmonic colour fits with the possibility that Schoenberg had a basic chromatic symmetry with considerable nineteenth-century provenance in mind, with F sharp and B flat important tonal centres in the work a major third above and below the main tonic of D. However, since D major's role in instantly transforming the mood of the music from apprehensive and unstable into affirmative and even exuberant is going to be clear from the very outset of the extended Stanza 4 episode representing the man's comforting and inspiriting words to his lover, the need to convey a sense of the momentous psychological significance of this event presented Schoenberg with a considerable challenge – to avoid the initial banality of obviousness, and also to avoid a feeling of the anticlimactic in the continuation, when as the poem indicates there is no longer any sense of anxiety or insecurity between the lovers. It is true that they might be aware that they will still need to steel themselves to face criticism and even condemnation from the people around them, and it is the air of euphoric confidence in the special power of love that will give the work's ecstatic final stages its aura of affinity with Wagner's supremely enraptured Tristan and Isolde and transforms *Verklärte Nacht* into an unambiguously upbeat example of Night Music. It is almost as if, for both Dehmel and Schoenberg, such a happy outcome during daylight hours would have been unthinkable.

Sudden, precarious silences have featured already in the sextet, especially when cadences impend, but change and continuation rather than closure are required. In literalist vein, one might suppose that the five instances of a beat's silence before the man begins his response represent not just pause for thought but genuine hesitancy in face of the momentous decision he has taken. As it is, the rich D major chord and the solemn, hymn-like theme from bar 229 sound magnanimous to a fault, and it is only when the continuation begins to flow and acquire decorative elaborations, displacing the sententiousness with a romantic fervour that is almost too good to be true, that the music regains its momentum. It is important to remember here that in the autumn of 1899 Schoenberg was just twenty-five and, as far as we know, seriously in love for the first time. He certainly cannot be accused of understating the real moment of change, both formal and expressive, which his chosen poetic source material calls for.

In the abstract, the hypothetical tonic of the Stanza 4 music, B flat, proves to be the proper dominant of the actual tonic, E flat (minor). But the music twice pauses for thought (bars 218–21) on an arpeggiated diminished seventh that, with an added F in the bass, would become a straightforward dominant ninth in B flat minor (Example 2.6, bars 216–22). After the second of these comes the strongest instance of Wagnerian 'rhetorical dialectics'; a musical leap of faith, perhaps, treating the E flat and G flat of the diminished seventh as chordal notes and moving from A natural to B flat to provide a resolution of E flat minor. The first two statements of this chord are very soft and inflect it with a D which is about to return as the work's most basic centre of gravity.

Example 2.6 Schoenberg, *Verklärte Nacht* Op. 4, bars 216–22

The third and final statement is more firmly rooted, but Schoenberg then uses a sustained solo B flat (2nd cello) – what might have been the tonic of this section after all – to take the small step onto the dominant of D major in bar 229, lifting the curtain on Stanza 4 and at long last allowing the reassuring male voice to be heard.

Conformity to Dehmel's basic scheme would of course require that only in the brief concluding Stanza 5 section should actual dialogue between the characters be expected, and Schoenberg seems to make a particular point of allowing for 'his' and 'her' alternations of salient motives, as with Cello 1 and Viola 1 from bar 370. Nevertheless, the climactic, euphoric function of Stanza 4 can hardly be conveyed by treating the sextet as some kind of 'solo with accompaniment' texture, and such imitative, echoing aspects are no less prominent here. It is perhaps not too fanciful to think of these final stages (and perhaps the whole work) more as a 'dialogue' between the poet/composer narrator and the pair of lovers whose emerging unity of purpose is charted by Dehmel. However, the musical mood is characterised here, the texture is predominantly 'dialogic' in the sense of contrapuntal, and the overly sententious, hymn-like beginning of the man's response in Stanza 4 soon relaxes and expands into something less churchy, more romantic. The plethora of arpeggiated figuration, and the over-emphatic combination of arpeggios and rapid scales at a later stage (e.g. from bar 316), along with the persistent use of sequential repetition, are precisely the kind of romantic conventions that Schoenberg would soon seek to consign to a pre-post-tonal and pre-expressionist past, as mindless note-spinning for cheap emotional effect (Korngoldian Hollywood waiting in the wings?). He might also have cringed in later years at uninflected tonal sidestepping, like the move from the D dominant in bar 319 to the D flat major tonic in bar 320, the kind of consonant slippage which emancipation of the dissonance and the consistent suspension of diatonicism would soon render unthinkable. Such decadent swerves, after 1900, could be left to Richard Strauss – they would still be much in evidence in his operatic swansong *Capriccio* (1940–1). Nevertheless, the final pair of destabilised perfect cadences in D – at the end of Stanza 4 (bars 365–70) and just before Stanza 5's own coda (Example 2.7, bars 394–400) – have an expressive immediacy and intensity that underline the particular dramatic power inhering in traditional tonal techniques. Post-tonal, modernist symphonic and dramatic music would have to rethink its foundations if it was to find workable ways of matching such qualities.

Example 2.7 Schoenberg, *Verklärte Nacht* Op. 4, bars 394–400

Walter Frisch's analysis does full justice to the subtlety with which Schoenberg keeps his repertoire of short thematic motifs in play throughout the later stages of *Verklärte Nacht*; so thoroughly is the spirit of the music transformed that by the end of Stanza 4 even the 'walking' motif in its chromatic form is entirely free of the foreboding and fearfulness it spoke of at the beginning. Similarly, in bars 394–5 the accepted dissonances that had initially signalled all that was dark and doom-laden about the scene lead into redemptive resolution, *dolcissimo*, after which the chromatic continuations have more of an erotic frisson than the aura of moral condemnation they originally implied. *Verklärte Nacht* does not end with a focus on the lovers and their common purpose. The music is more evocative of the harmony of nature in the form of a moonlit wood which – even if the trees are leafless – can be imagined by the lovers as rustling (murmuring) in a summer breeze, perhaps as a prelude to the kind of resplendent dawn that will end *Gurrelieder*. Such transparently upbeat endings would not be possible in Schoenberg's post-tonal idiom, when even the most decisive final cadences (as in the Variations for Orchestra and the Piano Concerto) retain that sense of struggle which seems inevitable when dissonance is the new norm. In theory, post-tonal symmetries might have as much of a capacity for stability as the hierarchies in traditional tonal textures. But Schoenberg (unlike his pupil Webern) could never completely deprive his music of the elements that seem to suspend significant echoes from the past rather than completely suppress them.

Notes

1. H. H. Stuckenschmidt, *Arnold Schoenberg: His Life, World and Work*, tr. Humphrey Searle (London: John Calder, 1977), 39–40.
2. Walter Frisch, *The Early Works of Arnold Schoenberg: 1891–1908* (Berkeley: University of California Press, 1993). Further page references in text.
3. Bojan Bujić, *Arnold Schoenberg* (New York: Phaidon, 2011), 33.
4. *Arnold Schoenberg Letters*, ed. Erwin Stein (London: Faber & Faber, 1974), 35–6. Robert Vilain, 'Schoenberg and German Poetry', in *Schoenberg and Words: The Modernist Years*, ed. Charlotte M. Cross and Russell A. Berman (New York: Garland Publishing, 2000), 1–30 (11), citing Vilain's own translation of Dehmel's 'Principles of Lyric Declamation' (1906). Further page references to Vilain in text.
5. For an account of Wagner's essay 'On the Application of Music to the Drama' (1879), with full information about the original German publication, see Arnold Whittall, 'Über die Anwendung der Musik

auf das Drama', in *The Cambridge Wagner Encyclopedia*, ed. Nicholas Vazonyi (Cambridge: Cambridge University Press, 2013), 603–4.

6. Frisch, *Early Works*, 79. Further page references in text.
7. Mark D. Markowitz, *Alexander Zemlinsky: A Lyric Symphony* (Woodbridge: The Boydell Press, 2010), 51.
8. Frisch has provided a complete translation of 'Schoenberg's Music', Webern's 1912 essay, in the symposium *Schoenberg and His World*, ed. Walter Frisch (Princeton, NJ: Princeton University Press, 1999), 210–30.
9. Arnold Schoenberg, *Structural Functions of Harmony*, 2nd ed., ed. Leonard Stein (New York: Norton, 1969), chapter X (76–113).
10. As the consultant editor for Boss's work at Cambridge University Press, I have been able to study what is likely to be the final version of his *Verklärte Nacht* analysis, and I am extremely grateful to him for letting me see this in advance. However, there are no quotations from it here, and my own narrative remains more generalised and impressionistic than Boss's intricate graphic analysis with commentary.

3

BEFORE *ERWARTUNG*

Matters of Context

Verklärte Nacht had been written without commission, and without any promise of early performance, yet Schoenberg must have felt euphoric at having completed such an elaborate and intense composition so speedily, and he began to explore ambitious plans for an opera in its wake. Bryan Simms mentions 'three incomplete opera projects' which 'probably date from around 1901. *Odoakar* was squarely in the heroic Wagnerian vein. *Aberglaube* addressed the conflict between spiritual and physical love, and *Die Schildbürger* ... was a folk comedy.'[1] Making no significant progress with any of these, Schoenberg then decided to develop what had begun as a piano-accompanied song cycle using German translations of Danish poems by Jens Peter Jacobsen, intended for a competition, into an evening-length music drama for concert performance.

Whether or not this transformation was the result of missing the competition deadline with the original songs, or of not entering the competition because of Zemlinsky's view that he was unlikely to win it (Zemlinsky was apparently involved as a judge), Frisch and others have concluded that *Gurrelieder*'s transformation 'must have occurred within a short span of time in the spring of 1900'.[2] As with the idea of *Verklärte Nacht* as a generic hybrid – string sextet and tone poem – the even more striking notion of *Gurrelieder* as a music drama without staging – a kind of anti-*Gesamtkunstwerk* – made rapid progress between March 1900 and August 1902, when the orchestration of Part 1 and most of Part 2 was completed. That *Gurrelieder* was then shelved until 1910–11, to prepare for a premiere in 1913, probably had more to do with Schoenberg's increasing doubts that such a mammoth enterprise could be adequately performed in the short term than with any feeling that its musical idiom was coming to seem passé. *Gurrelieder* boldly resolved the principal problem facing new musico-dramatic composers around the turn of the century – how to avoid pale imitations of Wagnerian prototypes. As Kevin Karnes interprets it, Schoenberg found a 'deeply human' way of moving beyond Wagner's Tristanesque 'vision of redemption', whose main problem was 'that the transcendent love in which it was grounded seemed all but impossible to realize in practice' (146):[3]

Schoenberg lifted the veil of metaphysical illusion. In its place, he offered a vision of redemption grounded in recognizing one's essential likeness with – one's essential belonging within – the surrounding natural world. In contrast to those visions glimpsed in the work of Schopenhauer and Wagner, Schoenberg's was realisable in nothing more unattainable than a change in one's outlook on one's life. His vision . . . was deeply human. (161)

Put this way, there seems to be a good deal in common between Schoenberg's 'vision' at the end of *Gurrelieder* and what Charles Youmans describes as the 'post-metaphysical', Nietzschean ethos of Richard Strauss's 'artistic practice'.[4] Karnes reiterates his understanding that, after the trauma of Tove's murder as recounted by the Wood Dove, 'Schoenberg offers his listeners a redemptive vision of his own: of transcendence of suffering not through death but through personal identification with the natural world and its eternally recurring processes' (151). As Steven Vande Mortele observes, 'the tragic story of Waldemar and Tove is turned into a cosmic triumph of light over darkness and an all-encompassing, vitalistic ode to nature'; yet 'during the years between the composition of Part 1 of *Gurrelieder* and the completion of the entire work, it was the traumatized musical world of the "Song of the Wood Dove" that he would further explore'.[5]

The Wood Dove's song has particularly haunting connections with the musico-dramatic version of threnody or lament used to overwhelming effect by Wagner in Waltraute's narration in Act 1 of *Götterdämmerung*. As an important compositional genre dominated by expressions of darkness and despair, the lament might justifiably be thought of as a kind of Night Music by proxy. In a resourceful analysis, Vande Mortele highlights the special function of what he terms the Wood Dove Chord (a half-diminished seventh, or a major third on top of two minor thirds, as is Wagner's 'Tristan' chord) as 'more than merely a surface symbol for trauma. As a dissonance that occupies the place of the tonic, it traumatises the music's entire structure' (76), threatening and decisively undermining the music's tonal stability; and as he worked to complete *Gurrelieder*'s orchestration in the months after his composition of *Erwartung*, Schoenberg could scarcely not have pondered the irony of just how much more graphically he had been using dissonant, post-tonal harmonic formations to dramatise trauma in his 1909 monodrama than had been the case when actually composing the Wood Dove's song back in 1902. More than that, in 1909 he had sought to justify and find music for a dramatic, psychological trajectory that turned decisively against the upbeat endings of *Verklärte Nacht* and *Gurrelieder*, and even against the less stable but still consolatory resolutions of the second string quartet. Like the 'Song of the Wood Dove', when taken in isolation, *Erwartung* gives no hint of any 'cosmic triumph of light over darkness', and in later years, Schoenberg's exploration of transcendence and spirituality would have little use for 'vitalistic ode[s] to nature'. As a sub-category of Nature Music, Night Music would in turn be discounted, as Schoenberg's thinking about how music could and should devise techniques of problem-solving that might have theological or political rather than merely psychological overtones evolved. But such lofty heights were a long way off in the early twentieth-century years.

Teaching Classicism, Composing Expressionism

Between the completion of the string sextet and its first performance more than two years later, on 18 March 1902, there was a clear division in Schoenberg's life, between creative work on *Gurrelieder* and the choir training and operetta scoring that earned him some money. He also spent a few months (December 1901–July 1902) in Berlin as the music director of Ernst von Wolzogen's Überbrettl cabaret company and stayed on in the city for another year: having met Richard Strauss in April 1902, he set *Gurrelieder* aside in order to follow

Strauss's suggestion of composing a work using Maeterlinck's drama *Pelléas et Mélisande*. On the evidence of the score of *Verklärte Nacht*, as well as what was available of *Gurrelieder*, Strauss was impressed enough to recommend Schoenberg for a scholarship – the Liszt Stipendium – administered in Berlin by the composer and conductor Max von Schillings. Strauss, now rising forty and just beginning to make his own mark in the field of opera, must have felt that Schoenberg had the potential to create a more forthrightly romantic treatment of the story than Debussy had done (his *Pelléas* had been premiered in Paris that same year). Schoenberg completed his tone poem in February 1903, and despite having been taken on by a Berlin publisher – Dreililien Verlag – for the first time, and also having his Stipendium renewed for a second year, he decided to return to Vienna in July 1903.

Chamber music for strings had provided Schoenberg with his most satisfying early experiences as a practical musician, yet Vienna in 1903 was a city where the sounds of Brahms, Wagner, Strauss and Mahler brought special prestige to symphonic and operatic music. With *Verklärte Nacht*, Schoenberg had clearly sought to avoid the 'bleeding-chunk' effect of the kind of forthrightly quasi-operatic response to the Dehmel text provided by Oskar Fried in 1901. As a single-movement chamber work with a programmatic title, *Verklärte Nacht* boldly asserted claims to generic novelty, yet the virtuosity and detailed crafting of its textural counterpoint proclaimed a relatively traditional commitment to technical mastery as the crucial corollary of aesthetic inspiration. After completing it, Schoenberg seemed set on a stylistic path that allowed him to emulate aspects of Mahler, Strauss and Zemlinsky while bringing into ever-clearer focus the distinctive qualities of his own still-evolving compositional voice, most apparent around 1903 in his management of what amounted to hybrid formal designs in the sextet's allusions to symphonic poem and *Gurrelieder*'s to music drama.

While Schoenberg in his late twenties might also have hoped to follow Mahler, Strauss and Zemlinsky in building a successful career that combined composing and conducting, his turn to teaching suggested an instinctive awareness that his path had to be significantly different from theirs. After 1900, he soon became an efficient conductor, mainly of his own works, but opportunities to teach, either privately or within institutions, were clearly more useful to him (and not least in advancing the time when he could afford to give up hackwork for music publishers) than invitations to embark on the hazardous process of establishing a career in conducting. Between 1903 and 1911, he would not only belie his self-taught status as a composer by demonstrating special pedagogical skills in those purely academic routines of harmony, counterpoint and *Formenlehre* which he believed that all potential composers with genuine talent needed to master; he would also find time to put together his *Theory of Harmony* ('Harmonielehre'), a substantial treatise (first published in 1911 and dedicated 'to the hallowed memory of Gustav Mahler', who died earlier in that year) that emulated many earlier technical texts in tracing harmonic theory from its roots in tonality and functional harmony to freer, more complex elements 'at the frontiers of tonality', as his fifteenth chapter called it.

Schoenberg's ability to attract students with the capacity to pursue traditional kinds of academic study while beginning to compose radically – even anti-traditionally, as with Webern – heightened his sense of the need to take the lead in showing the true consequences of thinking through and beyond the innovations of Wagner and the other late romantic progressives – not just extending but, as he understood it, 'suspending' tonality as an unambiguously predominant single key, in favour of 'pantonal' allusions to two or more keys, whose actual tonic chords did not even need to be present. The consequence – especially intense in Germany and Austria – was a new aesthetic, significantly different from the romanticism that had dominated most of the previous century. The dream-like, often nightmarish perspectives of expressionism emerged in music alongside equally radical developments in painting (Kokoschka and Kandinsky) and poetry (Stefan George and Trakl); and these new perspectives would soon be closely linked to the human traumas exposed in Freudian psychoanalysis, as well as to a kind of Night Music that could easily appear to represent the experience of nightmare as a form of madness, the extreme opposite of the comforting nocturnal qualities embodied in the vocal or instrumental lullabies that many romantic composers had produced. Schoenberg's first short opera, *Erwartung* (1909), might not manage complete and utter independence of all the more mainstream music dramas of the time – it is often compared with Strauss's hyper-decadent *Salome* (1905) – but it is poles apart from the skilful mixture of menace and comfort found in the Night Music episodes of one of the most successful late romantic German operas, Humperdinck's *Hansel und Gretel* (1892).

In considering how best to engage with opera as a genre without compromising his emerging radical principles, Schoenberg would surely have become aware that the kind of successful mainstream contributions to post-Wagnerian music drama after 1900, not just by Strauss but by Pfitzner, Schreker, and even his friend Zemlinsky, retained more of the late romantic glitter and extravagance, often naturalistic rather than surrealistic in tone, than he himself was comfortable with, having made his own use of such an idiom in *Gurrelieder*. Schoenberg's often-uneasy relationships with his most talented and original pupils is well known, and that with Alban Berg might well have been even more fraught had Berg's remarkable success with an uncompromisingly expressionistic, post-tonal opera *Wozzeck* (which Berg began in 1914) been completed and premiered more expeditiously than was in fact the case. But it was not completed until 1922 and was first performed in 1925, a year after *Erwartung*'s premiere in Prague.

Between 1903 and 1907, Schoenberg's principal compositions include the Eight Songs for Voice and Piano Op. 6, the String Quartet No. 1 Op. 7, and the Chamber Symphony No. 1 Op. 9 (completed in July 1906 and first performed on 8 February the following year) – all impressive deepenings and intensifications of the technical qualities present in *Verklärte Nacht* and *Pelleas und Melisande*. Over the next two years, a complex sequence of events concerning both life and work unfolded, in which his distance in style and technique from Mahler, Strauss and Zemlinsky became ever clearer. By the end of 1909, Schoenberg had completed no fewer than five of his most innovative works – String Quartet No. 2 Op. 10, Three Piano Pieces Op. 11, *Das Buch der hängenden Gärten* Op. 15, Five Pieces for Orchestra Op. 16 and *Erwartung* Op. 17.

The Webern Effect

Commentators on Schoenberg who give pride of place to the radical technical developments in his music between 1906 and 1909 may wisely shy away from any suggestion that those developments were directly determined by the exceptionally turbulent series of events in his personal and professional life between his late twenties and mid-thirties. Having encountered both Strauss and Busoni in Berlin, he first met Mahler after his return to Vienna (he had known Alma Schindler, Mahler's wife, since 1900); in 1903, he also began teaching, first at a school run by Dr Eugenie Schwarzwald, where his students included Egon Wellesz. His high reputation as a teacher grew apace, and he began to attract private pupils of exceptional talent and ambition, Anton Webern and Alban Berg among them. At the same time, he developed contracts with prominent and progressive figures in the other arts, notably the architect Adolf Loos (who helped to promote several early Schoenberg performances) and, in 1907, the painter Richard Gerstl, who had moved into the same apartment block and was soon advising Schoenberg about his own forays into expressionistic painting. Schoenberg was interested in portraiture, as a possible way of supplementing his still-meagre income: however, apart from one striking portrait of Berg and another of Gerstl, his paintings were mainly self-portraits. Gerstl himself was potentially a major talent, but within a year of their first encounter he had started an affair with Mathilde Schoenberg, and they moved away together, leaving Mathilde's two small children behind with their father. One of the most dramatic events in the composer's musical life, the wildly controversial premiere of the String Quartet No. 2 (21 December 1908), discussed in more detail below (pp. 47–8), took place alongside the crisis which saw Mathilde Schoenberg persuaded (by Webern, among others) to return to her husband. Gerstl subsequently killed himself on 4 November 1908.

Webern was twenty-five in 1908 and had met his own fiancée in 1905; they eventually married in 1911. His role as close family friend as well as student of Schoenberg seemed to highlight the strong contrasts in character between master and pupil. A Catholic from birth, and entitled to use the honorific 'von', Webern's right-wing sympathies in the years after 1920 underline the irony of characterising him as musically more visionary than Schoenberg or Berg. In the 1950s and 1960s, helped by Stravinsky's enthusiasm for the twelve-tone works, and the persuasive performances conducted and recorded by Pierre Boulez, he attained a degree of posthumous celebrity. Yet the contrapuntal transparency and subtle spatial and structural symmetries of his atonal serialism began to reveal their limitations when the pantonal ambiguities of Berg and Schoenberg – especially when allied to strongly dramatic subject matter – became more influential on the still-evolving modernist mainstream after 1970.

Despite the often-abject deference and eagerness of his students to please, Schoenberg was notoriously captious about their character and competence, most startlingly perhaps in his later disparagement of one of the earliest, Egon Wellesz.[6] The Webern case is more complex and centres on the question of the degree to which, in the years around 1907–10, his ideas about the need not just to extend but to abandon classical tonal forms and traditional harmonic functions provoked Schoenberg himself to move forward more speedily and more intransigently than, in retrospect, he might have thought justified. However, even if decisive evidence were to emerge that Schoenberg was the reluctant accessory after the fact of Webern's root-and-branch advocacy of dissonant atonality, there is surely no question that the relevant works of Schoenberg's, up to and including *Pierrot lunaire* (1912), are bolder and more advanced as aesthetic as well as technical demonstrations of post-tonal potential than Webern's small-scale orchestral, instrumental and vocal works of the same period, accomplished and highly original though these certainly are – most notably, perhaps, the sets of Pieces for Orchestra Op. 6 (1909) and Op. 10 (1913). Similarly, it is difficult to claim that Schoenberg 'learned' the need to introduce and emphasise spiritual and religious themes (in contrast to the secular, erotic stresses of the years before 1913) from Webern, whose own introduction of such texts came after 1919. It was not until 1936, after his emigration to America, that Schoenberg showed his full awareness of his and Webern's consistently different approaches to post-tonal, twelve-tone composition, dedicating his own thoroughly unWebernian violin concerto to Webern, just as Webern had dedicated his thoroughly unSchoenbergian Concerto for Nine Instruments Op. 24 (1934) to Schoenberg. The kind of 'modernism without expressionism' found here can occasionally encourage commentators to dub Webern the most complete and innovative neoclassicist of the interwar years, despite the obvious contrast between a twelve-tone technique rich in invariant motivic and chordal elements and the forceful yet fragile tonal structures favoured by Bartók, Stravinsky and others. The progression from the explosive expressionist miniatures Webern composed before 1914 and the refined reticence of most of the twelve-tone works remains one of the most telling presentations of a specifically twentieth-century technical and aesthetic pilgrimage – a pilgrimage that Schoenberg also undertook, though to very different effect and in response to very different personal and professional circumstances.

Towards *Erwartung*: Compositional Concerns

During the years 1905–7, Schoenberg was not only able to complete three large-scale compositions, but also to have them performed without undue delay. The premiere of *Pelleas und Melisande*, which Schoenberg himself conducted, took place on 26 January 1905; then the String Quartet No. 1 (completed 26 September 1905) and first Chamber Symphony (completed 26 July 1906) – both single-movement structures – were first played in Vienna on 5 and 8 February 1907, respectively. Looking back on this time forty years later, Schoenberg seemed willing to admit that he had misunderstood his own position in July 1906: 'when I had finished my first *Kammersymphonie* Op. 9, I told my friends "Now I have established my style, I know now how I have to compose". But my next work showed a great deviation from this style: it was a first step towards my present style'. This is generally understood to mean that, in that 'next work', the String Quartet No. 2 Op. 10, 'the overwhelming multitude of dissonances cannot be counterbalanced any longer by occasional returns to such tonal triads as represent a key. It seemed inadequate to force a movement into the

Procrustean bed of a tonality without supporting it by harmonic progressions that pertain to it.'[7]

Here Schoenberg's abiding dilemma – how to speak of music that seemed to resist the essential characteristics of tonal composition without using that dread negative 'atonality' – is clear to see, and subsequent commentators have expended immense amounts of time and ingenuity debating whether the differences with respect to harmony and tonal structuring between the Chamber Symphony No. 1 and the String Quartet No. 2 are indeed as fundamental as the composer himself chose to believe. But differences of both tonal and expressive character are substantial and undeniable. While Op. 9 seems to chart a quasi-Straussian path of heroic struggle and reflection to achieve a forceful and triumphant, horn-resplendent resolution, Op. 10 – more Mahlerian than Straussian in spirit, to this extent – turns away from earthly, human perspectives, reaffirming at least some of those melancholic, nocturnal qualities that vie with an emerging awareness that aspirations to a transcendent spiritual advance could no longer be set aside. What Stefan George describes, in the pair of poems that Schoenberg chose for the last two movements of Op. 10, required sorrow and lament to be swept up into a sense of something beyond earthly existence – sensing that 'air from other planets' by way of music whose 'otherness' had to be palpable, yet which was voiced by Schoenberg in a style that moved to greater enrichment of a language preserving tonal perspectives. The new awareness of those 'other planets' was still rooted in life on earth.

Since the details of Mathilde Schoenberg's affair with Richard Gerstl in 1908 and the psychic turmoil displayed in the 'ethical will' drafted by Schoenberg that alludes to the George poem 'Entrückung' have become well known, the spirit of exalted bitterness that infuses the music of Op. 10 seems more transparent than ever.[8] The full negative force of Night Music may indeed be kept in check, even in the third movement's portrait of deep sorrow. But to judge from its response to the premiere, the experience of listening to Op. 10 as a whole had nightmarish qualities for the conservative Viennese audience assembled in the Bösendorfer Saal on 21 December 1908. The Quartet No. 2 is probably the best documented of all Schoenberg's compositions, and – apart from various first-hand reports on the near-riot that occurred on 21 December – it is fascinating to see the efforts from early annotators and reviewers sympathetic to Schoenberg to underline the audible, logical compositional processes that justified placing the work in a long and distinguished lineage extending from Haydn and Mozart to Beethoven and beyond.

The programme notes for the second performance, two months after the first on 25 February 1909, in which Zemlinsky seems to have had a hand, were doubtless designed in haste to deter uncomprehending hostility and riskily stress the argument that 'almost excessive consistency, rather than arbitrary wilfulness, governs here', and that 'the formal structure and motivic material in no way deviate from the "rules"' – as if 'the "rules"' were a tiresome inconvenience that no sensible person would take seriously. The technical narrative which follows in the notes is then entirely devoted to tracing thematic, motivic processes, and nothing is said about programmatic issues arising from the scherzo's references to 'Ach, du liebe Augustin' or the George texts.[9] But Schoenberg himself would doubtless have been angry and appalled if such notes had given any hint of the personal crisis that lay behind the music's character, as distinct from its craft, especially as the personal and musical consequences of that crisis would take considerably more time to work themselves out, well beyond the early days of 1909.

Points of No Return

Of the five major works completed by Schoenberg between 1899 and 1908, three (*Verklärte Nacht*, the first String Quartet and the first Chamber Symphony) end with firm and unambiguous emphasis on major triads representing the tonic chord of the governing tonality. One, *Pelleas und Melisande*, ends on the tonic minor, in keeping with the story's tragic conclusion; and one – the last – the second String Quartet, ends on an F sharp major triad, diminuendo, whose status as an afterthought correcting the F sharp minor triad that precedes it seems fitting for a work whose pair of vocal movements progress from a full-throated lament for the sufferings inherent in human life to a celebration of the joys of leaving behind earthbound stability and even human life itself. Instead of the affirmation of 'peace on earth' that seems inherent in the serenely resolving conclusions of *Verklärte Nacht* and the String Quartet No. 1, as well as Schoenberg's short choral work with that title (1907), or the uninhibited joyousness with which the first Chamber Symphony ends, the ending of the second quartet seems almost wearily to confess that 'peace' and 'earth' are incompatible, and that the 'old' kind of tonal cadence has finally lost its power to satisfy, convincingly and movingly – whereas the mysterious dissonance with which that final cadencing phase begins seems to embody something truly radical and expressive – a post-tonal trichord ([016] – G sharp, A, D) spatially spread out by doublings, and ready to assume a much more decisive role in subsequent works, when its mixture of perfect fifth and tritone would serve to pinpoint the uneasy conjunction between something formerly central and something newly fundamental. For example, the last right-hand trichord of the first song in *Das Buch der hängenden Gärten*, begun during March 1908, gives the same [016] collection as A, G sharp, D sharp. (The E sharp sustained below as bass note subtly reinforces the sense of a chord mixing major and minor thirds, enharmonically spelled as F, A flat, A natural, D flat. Another [016] collection forms the first left-hand chord of the piano piece Op. 11, No. 1.) (Example 3.1(a), (b), (c)).

At first glance, the poetic, quasi-spiritual image of 'transfiguration' ('Verklärung') in the poem by Richard Dehmel which inspired Schoenberg's string sextet of 1899 might appear to progress smoothly to the poetic image of 'Entrückung' in the poem with that title by Stefan George which Schoenberg set in the fourth movement of his second quartet; indeed, 'transfiguration' is one of many possible translations of the word listed by Severine Neff before she points out that Schoenberg's own preference was 'transport' (170). It is easy to assume that the two poets meant exactly the same thing by the word, yet before accepting that conclusion it is useful to consider Robert Vilain's reference to Julius Bab's comment, in 1909, that 'all serious connoisseurs of the arts in Germany are divided into those who admire Dehmel and

Example 3.1(a) Schoenberg, String Quartet No. 2, Op. 10, final five bars
(b) Schoenberg, *Das Buch der hängenden Gärten* Op. 15, No. 1, final five bars
(c) Schoenberg, Three Piano Pieces Op. 11, No. 1, first three bars

those who admire George'.[10] For Vilain himself, Schoenberg's ability to admire both presents a puzzle: 'while Dehmel was abjuring the traditional influences that produced neo-romantic or symbolist poetry in German, Stefan George and Hugo von Hofmannsthal were espousing them' (15). Nevertheless, just as

Dehmel's celebration of the happy ending to a very modern kind of interpersonal dilemma in *Verklärte Nacht* suited the young composer's euphoric discovery of romantic love in 1899, so 'the emotions depicted in this drama of desire and loss' – George's *Das Buch der hängenden Gärten* – matched his very different emotions nine years later. As Vilain sees it, 'Schoenberg's discovery of George ... had opened up a poetic world of strong but controlled emotion, characterised by great formal and ethical rigor and above all by loneliness and the need for renunciation' (20). In *Entrückung*, George 'describes the total dissolution of the poetic identity in sound and movement and its eventual reestablishment as a passive element of the greater spiritual whole' (30). This kind of visionary enunciation of an ecstatic yet solemn, solitary fulfilment very different from the domestic bliss envisioned in *Verklärte Nacht* seemed ideally appropriate for the technical outcome in Op. 10's finale, where tonality is impulsively renounced, then apprehensively reinstated as something which is, ultimately, fading and uncertain. As with the song cycle, it was not a case of George providing the troubled composer with reassurances about the value of stable conservatism, or traditional romanticism, but of the composer embracing the loneliness of a creative force intent on combining 'strong but controlled emotion' with 'great formal and ethical rigor' – a circumstance which appeals to analysts keen to demonstrate that Schoenberg's compositions from Op. 10 onwards already deploy a range of evolving and related pitch materials that lend themselves to description in terms of what amounts to a new theory of post-tonal composition, replacing the old principles of tonality. Yet in 1908, Schoenberg was still a long way from formulating what would eventually become the twelve-tone method; in Op. 10 and Op. 15, images of darkness and apprehensions of nightmare coexist with aspirations to a state of transfiguration not yet achieved, but conceivable if the right spiritual (religious, ethical) path were found and followed.

In 1908, as the Mathilde–Gerstl crisis was reaching its conclusion, Schoenberg's compositional work remained far removed from Webernian miniaturism. As well as completing the second quartet, he made a start on a second chamber symphony (left unfinished – continued and completed as late as 1939) and also on a dramatic vocal work that would eventually become *Die glückliche Hand* Op. 18, although this would not be finished until 1913. Of more immediate concern was the collection of fifteen Stefan George settings, *Das Buch der hängenden Gärten*, whose completion on 28 February 1909 presaged a great explosion of creative activity with Night Music at its heart – the Three Piano Pieces Op. 11 (February, then August 1909), Five Orchestral Pieces Op. 16 (May–August 1909) and the monodrama *Erwartung* Op. 17 (August–October 1909).

This was a time of great extremes for Schoenberg. After the second string quartet echoed the radicalism of Beethoven's Ninth Symphony in abandoning purely instrumental constraints and highlighting the assertive fervour of the human voice, *Das Buch der hängenden Gärten* seemed determined to celebrate the continuing relevance of the kind of miniature music drama pioneered by Schubert, as a melancholy and ostracised protagonist (with just piano accompaniment) explores the depths of the poetic and psychological imagery provided by the texts, set with almost completely syllabic simplicity, and shunning the brief but powerful points of grandly operatic emphasis found in the Op. 10 settings. (Only in the fourth song of Op. 15 does a brief vocal glissando add a touch of dramatic rhetoric in what is otherwise a notably restrained but consistently intense lyricism – a *Winterreise* for the age of expressionism.)

Erwartung, Schoenberg's second major piece of night music is, like *Verklärte Nacht*, a single movement of around half an hour in length. Also like the sextet, it deals with a relationship between a married or cohabiting couple that is under severe strain, and this time irrevocable breakdown rather than reconciliation is the outcome. Schoenberg's propensity for projecting his own personal circumstances onto his compositional work has often been downplayed by commentators keen to highlight his purely technical progressiveness, and the associated assumption that mundane programmaticism must have been beneath the notice of a composer so high-mindedly wedded to moving music forwards into a truly modernist mode of expression. Such an assumption has

Example 3.2 Schoenberg, *Das Buch der hängenden Gärten* Op. 15, final ten bars

suffered several blows as a result of recent research, including the discovery that Schoenberg's first major instrumental work to have a purely generic title – the String Quartet No. 1 Op. 7 – had a 'very definite – but private' programme beginning with states of 'rebellion, defiance, longing and rapture' and ending with a 'homecoming . . . quiet joy and the contemplation of rest and harmony'.[11] Clearly this 'darkness to light' trajectory is not so different from the basic scenarios of *Verklärte Nacht* or *Gurrelieder* and confirms the obsessiveness of Schoenberg's commitment to this form of psychological pilgrimage as a governing 'Musical Idea'. But Schoenberg's actual experience of domestic crisis in 1908 coincided with compositions that had rather less affirmative endings: the second quartet's last-minute change from minor to major tonic triad is in a context where fundamental instabilities remain unresolved, and *Das Buch der hängenden Gärten* reinforces its prevailing uneasiness and pessimism rather than alleviating them, as the composer seemed to grow increasingly dissatisfied with upbeat conclusions affirming tonal unity and major-key consonance. A starkly decisive D minor ending is perfectly possible, but Schoenberg decides that it is unnecessary, undesirable, a false rounding-off of moods and thoughts that demand something more boldly inconclusive (Example 3.2).

Three Piano Pieces Op. 11 as Night Music

Between the first Chamber Symphony (completed early in 1906) and the sketches for Three Little Chamber Pieces (1910), the Three Piano Pieces Op. 11 are Schoenberg's only compositions without titles or known programmatic connections. Had Schoenberg decided to borrow the kind of titles chosen by Brahms for his later piano miniatures – Capriccio, Romanza, Rhapsody, for example – they could be neatly categorised as a consciously contrived farewell to Brahmsian romantic intimacy and ebullient poetic fantasy. Or else a more Lisztian heritage could be proposed in the first piece's 'Valse Oubliée', the second's 'Notturno', and the third's 'Danse Macabre'. Nevertheless, in 1909 any such hinting at a late romantic provenance would surely have emboldened the composer's critics to accuse him of a lack of confidence in his own innovatory zeal. As simply 'pieces', these were *sui generis*, and not to be bundled into historical categories he had no wish to evoke.

Considering Op. 11 as Night Music requires a perspective that does not confine itself to the basic question – 'Tonal oder Atonal?' – which Jack Boss chose as the title of his chapter on the first of the three pieces. Boss's first section heading – 'The complicated, contradictory nature of Schoenberg's middle period music (Op. 11, No. 1)' – signals that he is not likely to endorse the ambitions of those like Will Ogdon who proposed a comprehensive tonal explanation of a piece that 'opens in G major, with m.12 beginning an "episode" in E flat minor', and 'hears the closing measures as suggesting both G and E flat major simultaneously, although G has priority'.[12] Although Ogdon's reading has the potential to suggest an alignment with Schoenberg's own notion of suspended tonality, as expounded by Richard Kurth,[13] where a principal tonic (here G) is 'suspended' by an alternative (here E flat), Boss prefers a Schenkerian to a Schoenbergian understanding of tonal structure. By this criterion it is unquestionable that 'in Schoenberg's middle-period music ... tonality relinquishes its role as guarantor of large-scale coherence' in the form demonstrable by a Schenkerian voice-leading analysis. A feeling of convincing continuity and progress – an overall shape that is something more than a random compilation of separate smaller-scale events – is not enough, and the effort required even from expert listeners to hear Op. 11, No. 1 in Ogdon's terms does rather suggest a need to move consideration of the music into less rigidly formalised areas of generic association. Listening with closer attention to rhythm than to harmony could justify the argument that links with the waltz, as developed especially by Chopin and Brahms in the nineteenth century, help to strengthen the formal emphasis on the return, now in octaves, of the initial motif in bar 53, near the end. The piece might indeed be a 'suspended' waltz, a considered response or reaction to a traditional genre rather than a 'mechanical reproduction' of that genre. But there is enough consistency in the rhythmic patterning and phraseology to suggest that even if the constantly dissonant chording means that it cannot be tonal, it is not athematic or 'a-generic' either.

It is not Night Music, however. The febrile central section is capricious rather than nightmarish, and from a technical point of view it might best be regarded as a prelude to the main, nocturnal movement that follows it. If bar 58 is thought of as the 'real' ending of the first piece, with the G-based chord whose superstructure of thirds is similar (not identical) to the cadential chords of Op. 15, No. 5, bars 59 to 62 serve as a transition to the mood and material of the much longer second piece. Here, while individual chords may be as consistently dissonant (or 'a-diatonic') as those in the first piece, the initial emphasis on a pedal note and simple two-note ostinato which without the right-hand material could serve for a piece in F major or D minor shows that the Schoenbergian strategy of estrangement or suspension with respect to the familiar and the foundational is continuing. The Nocturne genre, as realised by Chopin, is in essence lyrical, quasi-vocal, with more than a hint of the flowering into florid Bellinian ornamentation of initially smooth and peaceful melody. Schoenberg in turn hints at a melody wholeheartedly operatic (even *Tristan*esque) in its arching, evolving phrases, distinctive in reaching beyond purely vocal registers and becoming part of chorale-like chords from time to time. However, despite the pianistic elaboration of the climax, with its cadenza-like decoration, this is arioso, musical prose, rather than poetic melody of the Bellinian type, and the mood meditative yet troubled, the music of a sleepless night, with the half-suppressed signs of a wakeful, restless person concerned not to disturb a sleeping partner. As part of his discussion of the staying power of tonal common practice in progressive music since 1900, Daniel Harrison considers Busoni's 'Konzertmässige Interpretation' of Op. 11/2, which 'applies traditional rhetorical devices to an originally emancipated-unto-anarchic harmonic environment, creating thereby at least a suggestion of traditional tonality if not a full-realized tonal center'.[14] Harrison feels that 'apart from some registral differences and passing intervallic inversion, no notes of Schoenberg's atonal original have been altered, but Busoni's "beautification" creates a startlingly traditional, even familiar sound world – yet depopulated of known consonances' (43). Part of that 'sound world' is the rhythmic-generic characterisation already emphasised here, the kind of characterisation that the much shorter, more turbulent third piece seems determined to demolish.

True to his own method, Jack Boss aims 'to show that, despite its fragmentary form, Op. 11, No. 3 is held together by something stronger than motivic networks, motive processes. In other words, its diachronic motive and chord progressions are not only connected, but also can be heard as generated by a small number of definable procedures'.[15] The consequent battle between the struggle for freedom and the determination to control might indeed be part of the listener's experience and help to reinforce the special character of the piece. Set against the element of domestic restraint that seems to govern the second piece's expressive world, No. 3 'reads' like a no-holds-barred shouting match, out in the open, with occasional touches of restraint, even pathos, that are always swept away in more forceful gesturing and assertive reiterations. This naturally has consequences for the piece's overall design, which does not conform to Schoenberg's usual template. As Boss puts it, 'Op. 11 No. 3, unlike its predecessors, does not have the profile of a complete musical idea'. Yet despite this difference, the piece 'is a masterpiece in the way it combines motivic and harmonic integration and a clear large organizational scheme with its strong expression of formal fragmentation and abruptness' (109).

And if this is evidence of the composer's conscious awareness that, for once, his habitual formal principle could not serve his needs on this occasion, all credit to him for recognising when flexibility needed to be more salient than routine. Op. 11, No. 3 is clearly not Night Music after the manner of Op. 11, No. 2: rather, with a vivid premonition of *Erwartung*'s agitated twists and turns, the second piece's prevalent unease and lyrical eloquence are transformed into the opposite kind of hectic, tersely dramatic outbursts, with predominantly despairing moods and the darkest and most destructive of thoughts.

'There Is Absolutely Nothing Symphonic about Them . . . '

As well as rounding off Op. 11 with the abrasively radical third piece in August 1909, Schoenberg completed the draft full scores of his Five Orchestral Pieces Op. 16 on 9 June, 15 June, 1 July, 18 July and 13 August 1909, respectively – all before beginning concentrated work on *Erwartung* on 27 August. Back in 1908, Richard Strauss had asked Schoenberg to send him 'a few (not too long) pieces' for possible performance by his Royal Opera Orchestra in Berlin, probably hoping for something stylistically along the lines of *Pelleas und Melisande*, if not *Verklärte Nacht*. As it was, the changes of style and technique that marked Schoenberg's development in the six years since the tone poem's completion sat ill with a composer who himself had changed considerably between completing *Elektra* in 1908 and beginning *Der Rosenkavalier* in 1909, and Strauss would have taken little comfort from a letter Schoenberg wrote to him in July 1909 (before the final piece was finished), saying that 'there is absolutely nothing symphonic about them, quite the opposite . . . no architecture, no construction. Purely a diverse, uninterrupted alternation of colours, rhythms, and moods.'[16]

This somewhat casual description does scant justice to aspects of thematic and harmonic connectedness which, if not 'symphonic' in the normal sense of that word, could hardly be thought of as lacking 'construction'. As for 'architecture', analysts have had no difficulty in tracing the presence of ternary designs, as well as generic allusions to fugue (No. 1), canon (No. 3) and, in the last piece, the waltz. Yet Op. 16 is not the straightforward premonition of Schoenberg's later neoclassical scores that such factors might suggest. Even before he succumbed to the blandishments of an anxious publisher, who requested descriptive titles, because 'compositions with the title "Pieces" don't get off the ground', he had told Strauss that the fifth Piece 'promised to be more cheerful than the "dark" Nos. 1 and 4'; and his chosen titles for No. 1 ('Premonitions') and No. 4 ('Peripeteia') acknowledged the Night Music moods of apprehensiveness and disorientation that proclaimed a basic difference from the uneasy nostalgia of No. 2 ('Past Things'), and the more mediative passivity of No. 3 ('Colours'). As for the 'more cheerful' No. 5, the rather enigmatic title – 'The Obligatory Recitative' – has set commentators a challenge which Schoenberg's own comments did little to ease, referring in his diary to 'a free form within nature, which is "obligatory" in the sense that only there can the ineffable be represented. One states the inexpressible in free form. In it one draws close to nature, which is also incomprehensible, but in effect all the same.' These observations are very much in the same spirit as Schoenberg's irritable response to his publisher when asked to provide titles:

music is fascinating because you can say everything so that the knowledgeable will understand it all, without having to give away your secrets, the secrets one does not even admit to oneself. Titles, however, give things away. Besides, the music has already said what there is to say. Why are words needed? If words were necessary, they would be there. Music says more than words.[17]

Required to provide words nevertheless, Bryan Simms offers a particularly useful view of 'The Obligatory Recitative': pointing out that Bach had used the term 'recitative' to describe the final section of his (purely instrumental) Toccata and Fugue in D minor, he says that 'like Bach's, Schoenberg's piece is an expressive masterpiece, a miniature *Carnaval*, in which our attention darts from one character to the next in a ballroom filled with whirling dancers' (81). Since Bach would become in many ways the genius presiding over Schoenberg's later works that focus directly on the 'ineffable' and even the 'incomprehensible', Simms's description indicates perhaps the most striking, least oppressive of Op. 16's premonitions. More immediately, however, aspects of the music's darker side connect potently with elements in Op. 11, Op. 15 and – above all – *Erwartung* Op. 17, where the ghostly presence of D minor would again materialise, if only briefly, along with other motivic features stemming from similar sources in Schoenberg's earlier, less intensely expressionistic back catalogue.

Notes

1. Bryan R. Simms, *The Atonal Music of Arnold Schoenberg, 1908–1923* (New York: Oxford University Press, 2000), 89. Further page references in text.
2. Walter Frisch, *The Early Works of Arnold Schoenberg, 1893–1908* (Berkeley: University of California Press, 1993), 142.
3. Kevin C. Karnes, *A Kingdom Not of This World: Wagner, the Arts, and Utopian Visions in Fin-de-Siècle Vienna* (New York: Oxford University Press, 2013), 146. Further page references in text.
4. Charles Youmans, *Richard Strauss's Orchestral Music and the German Intellectual Tradition: The Philosophical Roots of Musical Modernism* (Bloomington: Indiana University Press, 2005), 230.
5. Steven Vande Mortele, 'Murder, Trauma, and the Half-Diminished Seventh Chord in Schoenberg's "Song of the Wood Dove"', *Music Theory Spectrum* 39/1 (2017): 66–82 (81). Further page references in text.
6. See Bojan Bujić, *Arnold Schoenberg and Egon Wellesz: A Fraught Relationship* (London: Plumbago Books, 2020).
7. Arnold Schoenberg, 'On revient toujours' (1948), 108–10 (109); 'My evolution' (1949), 79–92 (86), in *Style and Idea: Selected Writings*, ed. Leonard Stein, trans. Leo Black (London: Faber & Faber, 1975).
8. For a translation with commentary, see Arnold Schoenberg, *The Second String Quartet in F sharp minor, Opus 10*, ed. Severine Neff (New York: Norton, 2006), 189–93. Further page references to this invaluable documentary volume are in the text.
9. Schoenberg, *The Second String Quartet*, ed. Neff, 250–68.
10. Robert Vilain, 'Schoenberg and German Poetry', in *Schoenberg and Words: The Modernist Years*, ed. Charlotte M. Cross and Russell A. Berman (New York: Garland, 2000), 1–30 (16). Further page references in text.
11. Arnold Schoenberg, 'Private Program for the First String Quartet (1904)', in *Schoenberg's Program Notes and Musical Analyses*, ed.

J. Daniel Jenkins (New York: Oxford University Press, 2016), 151–3.

12. Jack Boss, *Schoenberg's Atonal Music: Musical Idea, Basic Image, and Specters of Tonal Function* (Cambridge: Cambridge University Press, 2019), 21, n. 29, citing Will Ogdon, 'How Tonality Functions in Schoenberg's Opus 11, No. 1', *Journal of the Arnold Schoenberg Institute* 5/1 (1981): 168–81. Further page references to Boss in text.

13. Richard Kurth, 'Moments of Closure: Thoughts on the Suspension of Tonality in Schoenberg's Fourth Quartet and Trio', in *Music of My Future: the Schoenberg Quartets and Trio*, ed. Reinhold Brinkmann and Christoph Wolff (Cambridge, MA: Harvard University Press, 2000), 139–60.

14. Daniel Harrison, *Pieces of Tradition: An Analysis of Contemporary Tonal Music* (New York: Oxford University Press, 2016), 42. Further page references in text.

15. Boss, *Schoenberg's Atonal Music*, 81.

16. For citations from Schoenberg–Strauss correspondence, see Simms, *Atonal Music*, 72–3.

17. Simms, *Atonal Music*, 74.

4

ERWARTUNG

It may be a critical cliché to single out the special association between verbal and visual images of night and darkness and the capacity of post-tonal compositions to disrupt the strong and stable traditions of music rooted in tonal harmony. But identifying such an association is part of the common currency of many synoptic accounts of modern music, some of which celebrate the unsparingly truthful and penetrating results, while others bemoan such an emphasis on the dark and doom-laden in human life and the human psyche and mourn the loss of the life-affirming uplift that so many tonal masterworks of earlier centuries provide. There is a profound contrast between the confident defiance of marital convention embodied in the poem by Dehmel chosen by Schoenberg as the source for *Verklärte Nacht* and the failed relationship of the in some ways deranged female protagonist of *Erwartung*, composed a decade later; and this contrast can be paralleled by the apparent opposition between a nineteenth century musical language anchored securely and serenely to consonant tonality and a freely floating, intensely dissonant sonic fabric that ultimately dissolves into a centrifugally chromatic haze.

Textually, there is little in common, structurally and stylistically, between the disciplined poetic designs of Richard Dehmel or Stefan George and the tumbling stream-of-consciousness prose provided by Marie Pappenheim for the monodrama. Where Dehmel and Pappenheim coincide, at the outset of the 'Verklärte Nacht' poem and the *Erwartung* libretto, respectively, is not in direct verbal reference to the darkness of night, but in the scene-setting, scudding moonlight: for Dehmel, 'der Mond läuft mit, sie schaun hinein. / Der Mond läuft über hohe Eichen' ('The moon moves along, they gaze at it: the moon passes over tall oaks'); for Pappenheim, the setting involves 'Mondehelle Strassen und

Felder' ('Streets and fields lit by bright moonlight'), while in the early stages of her monologue, the Woman observes that, although the moonlight was bright earlier on, it is now fading ('in der Dämmerung'), is even somehow insane ('Entsetzen') . At the end of these respective texts, the positive intimacy of the sextet is shown, as 'zwei menschen gehn durch hohe, helle Nacht' ('Two people walk through the high, bright night'). The protagonist of *Erwartung*, by contrast, describes the night in remarkably personal terms: she is 'alone in my darkness', recalling in Isolde-like imagery 'dein Kuss wie einer Flammenzeichen in meiner Nacht' ('your kiss like a torch signalling in my darkness'). The stuttering extravagance of expressionism has replaced the poised yet flowery eloquence of late romanticism, as decisively as the richly affirmative D major consonance at the end of *Verklärte Nacht* is swept aside by *Erwartung*'s totally chromatic concluding dissolution.

With the completion of *Das Buch de hängenden Gärten* Op. 15 in February 1909, and concentrated work on the piano pieces Op. 11 and orchestral pieces Op. 16 between February and August 1909 (all within nine months of Mathilde's return home and the suicide of her lover Gerstl), the parallel between a turn to dissonant, post-tonal compositional conclusions and what can only have been an uneasy restoration of domestic harmony as part of an exceptionally hectic stream of creative activity indicates a highly febrile state of affairs for the composer, both personally and creatively. Bryan Simms has suggested that 'when Schoenberg joined his friends and family at a summer retreat in Steinakirchen am Forst at the end of June 1909, his confidence with the atonal style had reached an exuberant peak', and having completed Op. 11 and Op. 16 'with virtually no pause he then turned to a new challenge – composing opera'.[1] Yet both confidence and exuberance might well have rubbed shoulders with a kind of desperation, a need to find salvation in innovative composition and to try to exorcise real-life traumas by directly confronting them in a work of art. Maybe there was even an element of hoping that revisiting the tragic quality of the ending of *Pelleas und Melisande*, but using the new post-tonal rather than the old tonal sense of an ending, might do something to encourage the possibility of happiness in real life. Certain affinities between the D minor tendencies of the tone poem, and more allusive references to similar harmonic regions in some of the Op. 16 pieces as well as important details in *Erwartung* itself (discussed below, p. 46) may have strengthened this possibility.

As Simms reports, among the friends and family assembled at Steinakirchen that summer was the twenty-seven-year-old Marie Pappenheim, 'probably a distant relative of the Zemlinskys', who 'had moved to Vienna to study medicine', and whose 'efforts as an amateur writer were probably already known to Schoenberg through four poems that had been published under the pseudonym Marie Helm in 1906 in Karl Kraus's *Die Fackel*' (90). Over the past decade Schoenberg had made abortive attempts at four different opera projects – the three from 1901 listed earlier (p. 38), and a fourth in 1906, involving Gerhard Hauptmann's play *Und Pippa tanzt!* Schoenberg had sketched some music for this shortly after attending the Austrian premiere of Strauss's *Salome* in Graz in May 1906, and it is striking that 'the musical fragments that he composed for the beginning of the work also evoke the style of *Salome*'.[2] That influence can also be detected in the brash fanfares and languishing lyricism of the Chamber Symphony No. 1, completed in July 1906. But two years later, Schoenberg's radical changes in style had left the composer of *Salome* far behind, and the once-sympathetic Strauss had reacted with abusive incomprehension on being sent the newly composed orchestral pieces. There may still be a hint of Salome's unstable, wilful qualities in the protagonist of *Erwartung*, but Schoenberg's radically compressed, tonality-evading idiom in the monodrama is more a critique of Straussian rhetoric than a continuation of it.

Choosing a Librettist

Reminiscing in her eighties, more than half a century after the event, Marie Pappenheim recalled the composer's peremptory request for 'an opera text', apparently on any topic of the writer's choice, and what she produced, in three weeks during a summer stay with a different set of friends (not including Schoenberg) at Traunkirchen, and with a possibly unconscious allusion to the ambience of *Verklärte Nacht*, derived from 'her own fearful emotions experienced as she walked at night through a patch of dark woods'. In her much later recollections Pappenheim asserted that 'I received neither directions nor hints about what I should write, and I would not have accepted them anyway'.[3] The drafts of this text that survive include many amendments by both Pappenheim and Schoenberg, but these were not necessarily the result of actual discussion between composer and writer, and Schoenberg seems to have accepted without question Pappenheim's idea of a drama as a scena for a single character of relatively short duration. Indeed, some such specification might have been part of their initial discussion at Steinakirchen, as Schoenberg implied when he wrote in a letter to Busoni at this time that Pappenheim, 'acting on my suggestions, has conceived and formulated everything just as I envisaged it' (95). His abortive ideas for operas back in 1901, together with those doubts about how mainstream opera composers such as Pfitzner and Schreker were using the genre, seemed to ensure that Pappenheim's unusual way with compression as well as with continuity gave him just the right kind of material to work with.

As a clinician, and in line with emerging Freudian theory, Pappenheim might well have believed that hysteria and deviant behaviour in women might be more plausibly explained as a response to the abusive behaviour of a male partner than as the sole result of the woman's own congenitally unstable state. Having with *Die glückliche Hand* (first sketched just a week after the Gerstl suicide in November 1908) already begun to conceive his own text for a short drama in which a male protagonist struggles in a hostile environment that includes a deviant female, Schoenberg may have felt justified in that uniquely febrile time of the summer of 1909 in seeking a female librettist to depict a threatened female protagonist in what is in some ways a companion piece to the other (still-embryonic) short drama. Depending on how far his thinking about that work had progressed from its inception in 1908 – and it did not begin to assume its decisive shape until 1910 – he could even have given Pappenheim a sense of *Die glückliche Hand*'s extremely diverse dramaturgy, encouraging her to go to the opposite extreme. But was Schoenberg as truly at ease with the emancipation of women as he was with the emancipation of dissonance? Julie Brown is a musicologist who has brought an early twenty-first-century sensibility to an interpretation of the composer and his work that attaches special importance to convergences between Schoenberg's thinking and that of Otto Weininger (1880–1903), the short-lived, massively unstable Austrian writer whom Brown describes as associating hysteria in women with 'the "inherent" untruthfulness of Woman: hysterical Man is uncommon, but the illness is encouraged in Woman by her fundamental amorality, her divided personality'.[4]

Given the impossibility, a century and more later, of simply accepting and mapping such ideas onto Schoenberg's works for female voice during the crisis years of 1908–9, Brown struggles to argue the case that *Erwartung*:

> also gestures, like *Das Buch der hängenden Gärten*, towards a better state beyond the present one: the ever-present moon recalls its menacing counterpart in *Salome*, but also stands as a symbol of Woman and brings with it an association with transfiguring power; and the path is a symbol of the woman's blind gropings and lost way, but nevertheless suggests a route that is leading somewhere, perhaps somewhere better than the woman's present. (150–1)

One can readily sense that Schoenberg *in extremis* at his wife's behaviour might have associated Mathilde's desertion with the kind of inherent female traits explored by Weininger. How seriously he actually considered or evaluated Weininger's observations in finalising Pappenheim's text and writing the music is impossible to judge, but the sense of *Erwartung* as a drama to which ideas about psychology and psychoanalysis remain immensely relevant is reinforced in the analysis of the monodrama by Seth Brodsky.[5] *From 1989* is an immensely ambitious and wide-ranging exploration of the relevance of Lacanian psychoanalytic theory to musical compositions, not all of which were written at a time when some knowledge of Lacan and his work was possible. For this very reason, however, *Erwartung* can plausibly be proposed as the example of Schoenbergian Night Music which retains the greatest fascination and has the best potential for critical exploration more than a century after its creation.

The nightmarish stream of consciousness that is *Erwartung* might indeed be seen as a bold dismissal of 'madwoman' opera as it had recently been presented in *Salome*, a garish historical pageant revelling in its daring use of a biblical episode to provide maximum titillation. Yet the finished work is a good deal less ghoulish and garish that might have been the case. As Simms observes, 'Schoenberg ... shortened ghoulishly neurotic passages in the original [libretto] in which the Woman falls upon her lover's corpse, fondles it, and finally kisses it, actions that may have been a touch too close to Strauss's *Salome*'.[6] While there was a well-nigh documentary quality to Pappenheim's portrayal of psychic disturbance, Simms argues that the composer's changes to the text suggest that he had 'little interest' in it 'as a realistic study of hysteria'; and although it risks crassness to labour the documentary aspect in connection with the composer's own immediate family, it is surely the case that an opera about a deranged wife murdering her husband and then treating his corpse as a sexual object would have outraged Mathilde's family and friends, even those (like Webern) who sympathised with Schoenberg as a wronged and slighted spouse.

Schoenberg produced the initial short score of *Erwartung* (which, had not been commissioned by any opera company and would not be staged for another fifteen years) between 27 August and 2 September 1909, and a fair copy of the full score by 4 October. Given this remarkable speed, it is understandable that commentators have often fallen back on clichés like the suggestion that the work somehow 'wrote itself'; and there has been wide endorsement of O. W. Neighbour's sage conclusion in *The New Grove* that the music 'depends on a rationality beyond conscious control',[7] neatly implying that it was perfectly possible that something welling up from the composer's unconscious mind could nevertheless be far from an irrational, random outburst of disorganised anguish. *Erwartung* may not have been consciously conceived as a riposte to Strauss's extravagantly large-scale single-act *Salome*, or to its even more expressionistic successor *Elektra*, which was premiered in January 1909. However, while concentration and disorientation were the key features of a work whose format resolutely rejected the traditional musico-dramatic proportions that had played a part in Schoenberg's thinking while labouring on *Gurrelieder*, he remained faithful to an operatic tradition that celebrated the special lyrical and dramatic qualities of a soprano capable of convincing assumptions of the great heroic-tragic roles, in Bellini or Verdi as much as in Wagner or, as a very recent example, in Strauss. Without doubt, the electrifying power and – despite the sordid context – sublime artistic qualities of Salome's great final declaration threw down a formidable challenge to other composers at this time, and in both *Gurrelieder* and the String Quartet No. 2, Schoenberg had invested heavily in the post-Wagnerian emotional force of overtly dramatic music for a heroic soprano voice. Not even *Erwartung* would reject such rhetoric entirely; nor would it require the new kinds of vocal sound – *Sprechgesang* – that *Die glückliche Hand* and other relatively experimental works of these years would deploy a little later on. It is therefore appropriate that technical discussion of the music should often highlight the degree to which a lack of theatrical experimentalism in the setting and staging might be complemented by the remarkably innovative aspects of its compositional processes.

Explaining Radical Change

Anyone attempting to survey everything substantial that has been written about atonal, post-tonal and twelve-tone music composed between 1908 and the 1970s will be struck by the changes of terminology and vocabulary that gained ground during the later twentieth century, something well illustrated if we compare the account of *Erwartung* by Walter and Alexander Goehr, first published in 1957,[8] with that by Jack Boss, first published in 2019.[9] Like Schoenberg himself, the Goehrs continued to speak of chords and harmony as if their constituent intervals were the same as those of tonal chords and progressions – that is, major and minor seconds, thirds, sixths and sevenths, perfect or augmented fourths, perfect or diminished fifths. The difficulties created by the use of these designations, when the music is more chromatic than diatonic, more dissonant than consonant, seemed, and may still seem, acceptable and justified as a way of helping to highlight the huge differences in character between *Erwartung* on the one hand and *Tristan und Isolde* or *Verklärte Nacht* on the other. Nevertheless, the increasing systematisation of technical terminology, as so-called free atonality yielded to the consistently ordered and transposed pitch-class series-forms of twelve-tone music, facilitated a transformation in understanding and thinking (if not, exactly, in hearing): it became possible to argue that thinking and speaking of something called 'interval-class [ic] 5' rather than a 'perfect fourth' recognised that the element described no longer had the character and function of a perfect fourth in diatonic tonal music, and the designation of intervals between pitches by the use of a number indicating the total of semitones involved became known as 'integer notation'.[10]

There is no room here to pursue the full consequences of such a change, and no need, given the range of explanatory materials easily available electronically: and it is almost certainly easier for students in the 2020s, with no memory of a time when things were different, to appreciate the value of a terminology designed to elucidate what is new in post-tonal music rather than simply clinging to what remains of the old, however cumbersome and inconsistent the verbal result. What challenges such a cut-and-dried conclusion is the reality that neither Schoenberg himself, nor any of the composers in his immediate 'school', formulated a comprehensive theory involving integer notation during the early stages of post-tonal or twelve-tone composition. And even if the challenge is discounted – these were instinctively inspired composers, not slide-rule-wielding researchers – the disparity does rather underline a wider historical point. The systematically serial initiative which began to emerge from twelve-tone pitch serialism in the 1940s – even if compatible with the preservation of tonal fundamentals, so that incidental and often quite prominent references to tonalities still occurred – tended to move the resulting music even further away from mainstream accessibility, as (by and large) the history of modernist, classical composition since 1900 seems to confirm. From this perspective, the existential-cum-compositional crisis that Schoenberg lived through in 1908–9 subjected the fabric of coherent musical discourse to unprecedented strains, the character of which is clearly set out in the

Example 4.1 *Schoenberg, Das Buch der hängenden Gärten* Op. 15, No. 1, final two bars

various theoretical initiatives emerging around 1970, when dissatisfaction with the usages in writing like that of the Goehrs became particularly acute – at least in academic circles.

A good example of this change is provided by the first score extract, right at the beginning of Allen Forte's *The Structure of Atonal Music*, which shows the last two bars of the first song in Schoenberg's *Das Buch der hängenden Gärten* as an example of 'the occurrence of pitches in novel combinations' which characterises 'the repertory of atonal music' (Example 4.1).[11] Along with short extracts from Berg, Webern, Ives and Stravinsky, Forte offers two further Schoenberg examples in these introductory remarks: the first three piano chords from the George setting Op. 15, No. 6, and four 'occurrences of the initial theme' of the first of the Five Pieces for Orchestra Op. 16. Forte does not mention this piece's published title – 'Premonitions' – nor does he comment on the texts of the Op. 15 songs. Nevertheless, having stated at the start of his Preface that 'in 1908 a profound change in music was initiated when Arnold Schoenberg began composing his 'George Lieder' Op. 15. In this work he deliberately relinquished the traditional system of tonality, which had been the basis of musical syntax for the previous two hundred and fifty years', Forte was clear that none of the material discussed in his book was either twelve-tone or 'paratonal' – a term close to Schoenberg's own 'pantonal',[12] acknowledging the ambiguous terrain between tonal and atonal that Schoenberg's George Lieder and Orchestral Pieces were often felt by other analysts to inhabit.

Analysing pantonal music as if it were atonal is far from unproductive, since it provides a comprehensive yet manageably restricted terminology (pitch-class sets with integer notation) to identify both chords (simultaneities) and motivic elements; it also offers certain ideas about compositional process in terms of relations between such sets which can pinpoint the essential differences between music that has 'emancipated' dissonance at its heart and the functional identities and voice-leading principles suitable for tonal music, in which dissonance remains ultimately subordinate to consonance. When he reaches the final stage of his theoretical exposition, in a section entitled 'Set-Complex structures of larger scale', Forte returns to Schoenberg's Op. 16 pieces and discusses No. 3 with two main illustrations: a 'condensed score', representing 'the pitch content of the music' but not the orchestration, is followed by a graphic demonstration of set-class content geared to the kind of invariants and inclusion-relations which Forte's system prioritises.[13]

Such reduction to pitch-in-the-abstract, without the particular shades and shifts of instrumental colour which 'Farben' (Colours), Schoenberg's eventual title for the piece – a concession to the publishers, but significant nonetheless – indicates that he regarded as fundamental, not incidental, naturally encourages wide-ranging comparisons between the set-structure of the piece and as many other examples of atonal composition as are chosen to comprise the sample under analysis. For my purposes here, I favour emphasising the piece's exceptional qualities as a rare example of music by Schoenberg whose 'theme' is a chord fixing and sustaining a mood at the opposite extreme from the darker febrility that dominates his Night Music, and especially at the time when Op. 16 was composed. The piece's earlier title – 'Summer Morning by the Lake' – rather more pictorially explicit than 'Colours' – risked suggestions of escape and relief from doom and gloom that Schoenberg at that time had little inclination to encourage. Intriguingly, the pantonal quality of the piece's governing chord (Example 4.2(a)), poised between dissonance and consonance, has certain affinities with the sublime cadencing C major tonic (with added sixth) of *Das Lied von der Erde*, which Mahler was writing at the same time (Example 4.2(b)). But Schoenberg introduces a tension-creating conflation of A minor's tonic and dominant above the bass note C, something radically different from

Example 4.2 (a) Schoenberg, 'Farben' chord
(b) Mahler, 'Der Abschied', final chord

Mahler's concluding 'higher consonance'. Forte provides a virtuoso exposition of how the superimposition of distinct strata in 'Farben' further compromises any harmonic interpretation that seeks to rule out an overall atonality. Yet the substructural bedrock sustained from beginning to end enables the strangely passive spirit of the musical fabric to survive despite its vulnerability to the destabilising, fracturing forces that Schoenberg normally allowed to dominate, as his Night Music aesthetic required.

Perhaps Schoenberg in 1909 wanted his listeners to accept that Day Music or Morning Music, for all its apparent appeal, was simply not as 'real', as actively engaged in the drama of daily (and nightly) life, as the alternative. And if Schoenberg ever came to feel that the harmonic character of Op. 16, No. 3 was best defined not as atonality, but as suspended tonality – that is, 'floating' between the C major and A minor to which the components of its persistent chord allude, he never put that feeling into print. If pushed, he might have been prepared to argue that spelling out a pair of suspended tonalities in this way was too simplistic, and that it was better to suggest that pantonality – an unspecified range of possible tonalities – which a listener might sense without ever pinning them down or narrowing them down in the hierarchic manner tonal music traditionally relied on, was a safer option.

After the publication of *The Structure of Atonal Music*, the work of Allen Forte and other similarly orientated American music theorists – while provoking plenty of dissenters – also began to be taken on board in the UK and mainland Europe, where Schoenberg as troubled inheritor rather than intransigent rejector of all things classical and romantic was much more positively represented in the work of such writers as (in England) O. W. Neighbour and Hans Keller and (in Germany) Carl Dahlhaus. Dahlhaus was particularly influential as the result of a series of short essays with an unusually stimulating balance between broader aesthetic and historical issues (often citing the work of T. W. Adorno) and an analytical methodology deriving from close readings of Schoenberg's own texts, which were especially perceptive in their alertness to the composer's ambiguities and loose ends. With their vivid evocations of the actual experience of hearing (and, in the case of *Erwartung*, seeing) the works in question, Dahlhaus's writings are still well worth exploring,[14] and when first published helped to confirm convictions that, at the time of his birth centenary in 1974, Schoenberg was still very much a force to be reckoned with on the contemporary musical scene. In the UK, the successful staging of *Moses und Aron* at Covent Garden in 1965 brought Schoenberg into the musical mainstream, and while this work, along with pieces from the 1940s like *Ode to Napoleon*, the Piano Concerto and *A Survivor from Warsaw*, encouraged support for the view that Schoenberg's later compositions – some twelve-tone, others not – were indeed the best evidence of his evolution from incomprehensibility to accessibility, there was no shortage of performances of works from the Night Music years. *Pierrot lunaire* became a staple with the chamber group, formed by Harrison Birtwistle and Peter Maxwell Davies, which was initially called The Pierrot Players (later The Fires of London),[15] while with Pierre Boulez in post at the BBC, the largest-scale scores – *Gurrelieder, Die Jakobsleiter*, as well as *Moses und Aron* – were all performed and recorded. This was just at the time when a new, complete edition of Schoenberg's compositions, bolstered by volumes of commentary, and the assembly of the bulk of his original drafts and manuscripts in a single archive, initially in Los Angeles, later moving to Vienna, was being undertaken.

The frequent comparisons, from the 1920s onwards, between *Erwartung* and another – in some ways at least more conventional – expressionist opera, Berg's *Wozzeck* (first heard in 1925, and not begun until well after the completion of *Erwartung*), has led Glenn Watkins to reflect as follows:

the score of *Wozzeck* provides telling evidence of Berg's need to temper the agonies of a runaway Expressionism as epitomized by Schoenberg's *Erwartung* of 1909. Yet the solution Berg offers in *Wozzeck* was not so much a response to the hallucinations of Schoenberg's disoriented Woman stumbling over the dead body of her lover, or to its tonally unsettling music as it was a measured stocktaking, and an orderly reappraisal of its inner vision for a post-war world.[16]

Allen Shawn, focused more on aspects of individual psychology, observes that 'like *Wozzeck*, the woman in *Erwartung* is – in the heightened sensitivity of her anxiety – touchingly observant of the details of nature around her'.[17] In this way, the understandable eagerness of artists working after 1918 to involve the catastrophe and consequences of World War I in their work is pointedly contrasted with the much less socially and politically contextual-ised kind of expressionism that was emerging when *Erwartung* was written back in 1909, and in which the psychology of dramatic characters was much more inflected by individual sexual traumas than by the wider forms of exploitation and abuse endemic in decadent and especially militarised societies.

The Substance of *Erwartung*

Authoritative accounts of the genesis of *Erwartung*'s text and music inevitably reflect the feverish ambiguities of the completed monodrama. According to Bryan Simms, '*Erwartung* continues to guard its secrets',[18] and when it comes to the music, a basic opposition has arisen between those, like Ethan Haimo, who hear 'an opera ... in which there is not a single recurring theme or motive'[19] and those, like Jack Boss, who claim that 'motivic repetition is as important to the monodrama as it is in Schoenberg's earlier music'.[20] As the most recent and most exten-sive analysis, Boss's *Schoenberg's Atonal Music* (2019) chal-lenges listeners to perceive the coherence within a complexity and loss of control that is fundamental to the work's subject matter and character and argues that *Erwartung* is both pervasively thematic, even leitmotivic, and essentially atonal. Nevertheless, in the final stages (bar 411), Schoenberg cues a brief reference to an earlier song of his – 'Am Wegrand' (Op. 6, No. 5), written in October 1905 – and although at this point the song's D minor tonality is hinted at but then rejected, Boss shows how it is possible to trace connections between quite small details of the

Example 4.3 (a) Extract from bar 19 of 'Am Wegrand' (Op. 6, No. 5)
(b) The same pitch classes (reordered) at the beginning of *Erwartung*

song's materials and *Erwartung* from the very beginning. With a relatively slight degree of transformation, the tonal song's pair of minor thirds in bar 19, together with the lower D natural that comes between them (Example 4.3(a)), form part of the 'leading voice' (*Hauptstimme*) of *Erwartung*'s opening. The song's A flat and C flat, enharmonically transformed into G sharp and B natural, appear in the first bassoon, closely followed by A sharp, C sharp and D in the first oboe (Example 4.3(b)). Does this, and other possible allusions to 'Am Wegrand', which by no means accounts for all elements of the texture in these initial bars of the mono-drama, demonstrate the composer's conscious intent – perhaps to represent the deluded yearning for something stable and familiar that is now beyond reach? The fact that the analyst is contriving a signification here that is consciously derived from the song's music (but not dependent on its text, unlike the reference at bar 411) creates an assumption that such a connection was intended by the composer and was not the accidental product of a feverishly creative unconscious. However, even if such material thereby becomes 'leitmotivic' in Boss's interpretation, he is careful to note that Schoenberg is extending (or even in one way 'suspend-ing') rather than simply applying a Wagnerian trope: Schoenberg's 'impressionist themes (brief motives) and expressionist sonorities (set classes) to convey dramatic process' (222) are quite different from Wagner's boldly sculpted sonic signals – different also from

the prominent and recurrent thematic elements of *Verklärte Nacht*:
so it is open to individual readers and listeners to weigh up the pros
and cons of dealing with Schoenbergian complexity in this way.

Schoenberg himself had little to say about *Erwartung*, and this
serves to highlight the technical and expressive uniqueness of the
monodrama while enhancing its particular instability as something
so complex yet so rapidly executed that later on the composer
himself seemed torn between ignoring it and reliving the time of
its creation as he forged ahead with the task of calming the
whirlpools and thunderstorms of musical expressionism and light-
ening the darkness without attempting the impossible task of
banishing Night Music from a world in which a musical museum
culture was becoming evermore entrenched and more progressive
kinds of new music found it increasingly difficult to gain a hearing.
Most commentaries quote from a letter he wrote to Busoni three
days before beginning the composition, in which he declared in as
many words that he aimed to give his 'subconscious' free rein over
the constraints of conscious 'logic'.[21] In similar vein, historians
went through a phase of describing *Erwartung* and its close
contemporaries as examples of 'free atonality' – as distinct from
the 'strict' or orderly atonality of twelve-tone music from the
1920s onwards. But Jack Boss's analysis is more representative
of present-day thinking, with its assumption that Schoenberg's
'subconscious' was perfectly capable of offering him consistent,
even systematically ordered musical materials.

In the few words he eventually devoted to *Erwartung* in
the second edition of his *Theory of Harmony*, Schoenberg wrote
only about 'new harmonies' and the 'compulsion of a relentless
yet unconscious logic of harmonic design' to which his training
and temperament predisposed him – a logic which was likely to
have been more explicitly conscious when he was still composing
tonally. As an example, he argued that the eleven-note chord that
accumulates in bars 382–3 of the monodrama is articulated in such
a way that it can 'do little harm' even though 'the following
resolution' (onto a plain diminished seventh, diatonic in
B minor, shown in his example (Example 4.4)), which 'I believe
the ear expects', does not in fact occur.[22] Listeners capable of
expecting a diatonic if not consonant resolution in this context

Example 4.4 Schoenberg's hypothetical resolution of the eleven-note chord in
Erwartung, bars 382–3 (*Harmonielehre*, 2nd ed.)

might also be able to conceptualise the argument that the music at
this point is not atonal, even though a B minor tonality is not
diatonically, consonantly confirmed, but rather extended, or even
suspended, by its non-diatonic context. It would nevertheless be
difficult, if not impossible, to provide a listing of all the keys that
are extended or suspended, as opposed to entirely absent, in
Erwartung as a whole. Just as tonal music can convey a sense of
integration when its thematic materials reflect the prevailing intervals of the harmony – thirds, fifths and their inversions – so post-
tonal music can be understood (and heard) in terms of the shared
content of motives and 'simultaneities'.

Boss, with the full repertoire of post-tonal theory at his disposal,
finds logic, consistency and coherence not simply or even principally in vertically constructed 'harmonies', but in linearly projected motives – vertical and horizontal constructs both deducible
from the collection of prime form pitch-class sets held, after Forte,
to generate 'the structure of atonal music'. At first glance, as
mentioned earlier (p. 71), this analytical process appears to create
a gulf between the technical rationale for compositional choices
that result and what survives of Schoenberg's own understanding
of his objectives and methods. Schoenberg seems never to have
written (or, arguably, thought) about his music in the specific post-
tonal fashion adopted by Boss and many other music theorists
since the mid-twentieth century; and if something in him wanted
to ensure that the magic of *Erwartung* and other compositions
remained mysterious, there seems little point in attempts to align
compositional process with analytical interpretation. Only if we
choose to regard the composition and the analysis as complementary acts of problem-solving does a degree of alignment between

theory and practice begin to make sense: that is, if Schoenberg in 1909 successfully solved the problem of effective presentation of his magical, mysterious monodrama, the analyst – Jack Boss, in this case – has solved the problem of identifying the plausible working principles that underpin that success, even if these principles actually emerged ad hoc as the work rapidly committed itself to paper without the composer's unconscious mind requiring him to consider the universe of ordered or unordered pitch-class collections as an all-embracing system like that offered by Forte. Schoenberg might well (consciously) have relished responding to a text that begins with the protagonist declaring 'I cannot see the path', and ending with complete lack of conclusiveness – 'I was searching . . . ' – in the dark, the woman frozen in contemplation of a multitude of different paths and possible ways of escape, all with initial similarities, but pointing in radically different directions.

Managing so much information naturally leads to techniques of grouping and connectedness, as when Boss states that the four members of a particular set-class family not only 'often represent the lover's dead body directly', but 'typically occur when the text refers to darkness in general'.[23] In the case of one particular form of a family member – D, F, C sharp with the interval succession in semitones [3, 8] – Boss 'believes we are justified in claiming that' its 'gradual, incremental emergence as a significant motive through the opera's first 153 measures parallels and metaphorically represents her gradual, incremental discovery of his dead body' (191). Such insistence and emergence (whether consciously contrived or not) can also become increasingly audible to listeners, independent of the structural intricacies of their family relationships, contributing mightily to the mesmeric atmosphere of the monodrama. But mention of 'listeners' implies an easy accessibility of the music as sound (whether in live performance or recordings) which was hard to come by during the first half-century of *Erwartung*'s existence.

What to Listen For?

Central to the cultural ferment of the 1950s was a strong disparity between the determination of young avant-gardists to wipe clean the decadent slate of music as it had evolved over earlier centuries, and the conservative instincts of educationists confronted with calls to spell out exactly how such untraditional-sounding compositions as *The Rite of Spring* and *Wozzeck* were put together. When the Schoenberg pupil Walter Goehr and his composer son Alexander were asked to contribute a chapter on 'Arnold Schönberg's Development towards the Twelve-Note System' to a book called *European Music in the Twentieth Century* (first published in 1957), they were well aware that 'the first reaction upon hearing *Erwartung* is the very antithesis of the experience when listening to the perfection and apparent Apollonian symmetry of the eighteenth-century classicists', and that in *Erwartung* 'we experience a sense of being overwhelmed and lost in a mass of variation and juxtaposition of elements which are hardly memorable and result in a seeming structural incoherence'. Clearly, the critical method being deployed here is to set against a 'first reaction' the more considered reaction that should follow 'as we know the composition better', when 'we find that all these variants and "free associations" are well moulded into an overall shape and can be understood in a similar way to the works in the style of the preceding post-Wagnerian era'; and just as in those classical and post-Wagnerian works, from Haydn to Richard Strauss, 'the basic tonal principle of movement away from and towards a point or centre is retained',[24] thereby ensuring that 'a seeming structural incoherence' is indeed nothing of the kind, as the 'antithesis' of hearing *Erwartung* alongside earlier tonal music turns with experience into something broadly similar, if not literally the same.

Tempting though it is to encourage attempts to locate *Erwartung* and other examples of Schoenbergian Night Music within an integrated evolutionary progress, the consequent risks of downplaying essential instabilities and difficulties are considerable. Those 1950s avant-gardists coming to prominence around the time that the Goehrs' analysis was first published would naturally have bridled at this apparent denigration of a rare example of early twentieth-century radicalism; even Pierre Boulez, who – with the hindsight rooted in what he saw as the shamefully neoclassical retreat embodied in virtually all of Schoenberg's compositions after 1920 – judged that while hampered by a libretto that 'has dated terribly', and while also 'lacking the sheer formal elaboration' that Berg would achieve in *Wozzeck*, *Erwartung* demonstrates 'invention in a perpetual state of becoming, and freed from all predetermined formal frameworks'.[25] This form of words is strikingly similar to that which Boulez would also use to pinpoint what mattered to him about a much longer, earlier music drama, Wagner's *Parsifal*.[26] Indeed, the two extremes of *Erwartung* reception might be located in Boulez's later description of a 'large-scale structure' that is 'undetermined and indeterminate' on the one hand,[27] and in the Goehrs' narrative, predicated on the argument that 'the orchestral introduction ... makes a clear movement from G sharp through B natural to C sharp' on the other hand; and the fact that the first scene 'is clearly founded on a structure on which the notes C sharp and G sharp are predominant'[28] lays the basis for a continuation in which those particular pitches (especially the concluding C sharp) retain a degree of dominance until the very final bar. The Goehrs – riskily relying on asserting 'clarity' when the whole point in Schoenberg's mind might be to call clarity as usually understood into question – never go as far as to claim that *Erwartung* is somehow 'in' the key of C sharp overall and throughout. But it seems clear that most listeners are likely to find the music easier to understand in Boulez's terms than in the Goehrs', and especially if the aural experience convinces them that 'coherence' and the resulting aesthetic conviction is not necessarily the consequence of hierarchic ways of pitch organisation such as might link the tenuous pitch centralities of *Erwartung* to works undoubtedly 'in' C sharp like Beethoven's 'Moonlight' Sonata and the Op. 131 String Quartet.

In an essay first published in 1997, forty years after the collaboration with his father – 'he talked and showed, I wrote down' – Alexander Goehr said that when it came to *Erwartung*:

we only had the vocal score and the Mitropoulos recording, though he hired the full score from the publishers to check up on detail; most of the work was done by ear and at the piano. But what was observed in the study was original at the time, as it did not at all concern itself with motivic structures. ... My father picked out tonal characteristics (which he thought were probably unconscious and not deliberately worked out), such as long-term 'leading notes' and the emphasis on certain pitch levels at the beginnings and ends of phrases.[29]

The rest of the Goehrs' essay (in a particularly clear differentiation of its objectives from those of the Boss analysis) amounts to a sophisticated defence of harmonic, or even tonal, structuring in contemporary composition, as distinct from something predominantly motivic, whose possible limitations – including in Schoenberg's twelve-tone music – are then considered. That three-note cells as derivations rather than invariably literal repetitions of the same pitches are consciously deployed connectives in *Erwartung* is surely incontrovertible, and aural cognisance of these connections is probably the best way of achieving a sense of linear continuity analogous to that traditionally provided by the structural principles of tonality. But the predominantly atonal character of the monodrama is a vital indicator of its unusually radical identity, its apparent willingness to move towards a more avant-garde aesthetic (as Webern was exploring at this time) and in which the high modernist qualities of Schoenbergian expressionism could be seen as a passing phase before a relish for Night Music was decisively infiltrated by more metaphysical preoccupations.

Words Set to Music

It remains to be seen whether the initiative of the Boss analysis in proposing systematic (if also instinctive) structural and technical fundamentals for *Erwartung* will, when fully digested, decisively shift the emphasis of the monodrama's critical interpretation away from its polar opposite. Writing around the time of the Schoenberg birth centenary in 1974, Jim Samson described *Erwartung* as 'an astonishing instance of sustained musical invention, untrammelled by formal pattern, thematic development or repetition, and holding together only by the cohesive force of the composer's musical imagination and formal instinct allied to a pre-existing dramatic shape', and Samson quotes Willi Schuh, after attending the long-delayed premiere in 1924, describing a 'freely associative musical language': 'the only explanation of Schoenberg's sure-footedness amid the boundless immensities of his new musical realm is that he moulded this music as if obeying the compulsive dictates of his inner vision'.[30] A quarter-century after Samson, Daniel Albright was still writing of

a style of music that abolishes structures of musical development generated by pre-existing musical forms, in order to respond to the text with a kind of instantaneous immediacy; a style of music without any ballast of expectation, so that the listener never knows what will happen next. The German word 'Erwartung' means expectation, but since the music provides the listener with no predictive structure, expectation becomes a free-floating anxiety.[31]

Albright believes that 'for Schoenberg, the monologue of [librettist Marie] Pappenheim represented a halting speech so naked it had scarcely roused itself to the level of language, . . . a shattered, splintery sort of diction' that helps the composer

to investigate form at a level of improvisation almost unprecedented in art. . . . The text of *Erwartung* is all ellipsis; and the music is even more elliptical, in that it omits all the transitions that soften or condone the strange succession of chords full of major sevenths, or the melodic spikes that seem to represent pathological contractions of the heart through pathological contractions of the larynx. (149)

Giving musical expressionism a wholeheartedly physiological quality, Albright then acknowledges the valid points made by analysts who have found significant interrelations and even (varied) repetitions in the score; nevertheless, 'for the most part Schoenberg was faithful to his extraordinary, all-compassing hatred of repetition in music'. A little later, Albright reinforces his argument with the claim that, in writing *Erwartung* and other works of this period, Schoenberg's belief is that 'music does not set itself the task of constructing memorable units [like Wagner's *Leitmotive* and small-scale poetic-musical Periods, which often involve the use of sequential repetition to enhance memorability]; music instead sets itself the task of rendering the contours and discontinuities of a shifting subjectivity' (150).

    Allen Shawn is another significant commentator to have noted Schoenberg's deep unease with his own circumstances in 1909, and with the terrifying prospect that he would somehow be forced to write Night Music that dealt only in human despair and decadence. Shawn concludes that 'one of the keys to understanding Schoenberg's work in this phase is to see to what extent it is, despite superficial appearances, a continuation of tradition'.[32]

True to this ambition, he makes pointed comparisons: 'much as he had in his selections for *The Book of the Hanging Gardens*', Schoenberg's changes to Pappenheim's original text:

shifted attention away from clarity of narrative and towards the expression of emotions freed from their literal origins. From being a realistic study of the plight of a woman in a state of hysteria, a plight that might have been avoided had the woman been less emotionally tied to her lover, it became a more purely emotional expression of the unconscious mind. (94)

From the beginning, as Shawn sees it, citing Neighbour's *New Grove* account of Schoenberg's techniques, 'the independence of simultaneous musical events made possible by the lack of tonality permitted Schoenberg to present conflicting and "seemingly irreconcilable" textures and ideas at the same time, creating music that seemed to mirror the mind's own capacity for complex counterpoint' (96).

Finding the Way Forward

More pertinent, perhaps, is the possibility that Schoenberg was in search of 'somewhere better' for himself, or at least the *something* better that a change from 'the earthly to the metaphysical' might achieve. Noting that he also considered Pappenheim 'as librettist of a work based around Balzac's *Seraphita*, about an angel',[33] Julie Brown leaves open the possibility that the kind of aspirational voice so urgently projected in the setting of George's 'Entrückung' at the end of the String Quartet no. 2 was beginning to mark out a strand in the composer's creative thinking that would leave behind the Night Music emphasis of expressionism and early modernist psychodrama, as well as the 'post-metaphysical' perspectives evident in *Gurrelieder*.

Maybe in 1909 it was not even clear to Schoenberg whether that metaphysical strand should be Jewish or Christian, and not until 1912, in an oft-quoted letter to Richard Dehmel about his long-term desire 'to write an oratorio about modern man' who 'finally succeeds in finding God and becoming religious' did the ambition, and the apparently genuine connection to his own beliefs, begin to emerge, with an outlined agenda that would prove as elusive in the future as it was inescapable.[34] But by 1912, it was George's poetry rather than Dehmel's which better suited Schoenberg's increasing resistance to 'post-metaphysical' subject-matter, and it was the 'faith' marking out 'great men', rather than the mere 'conviction' of 'normal men', that should be determinedly aspired to.

By 1912, *Das Buch der hängenden Gärten* could also have seemed insufficiently experimental generically to suit Schoenberg's fragile mood of the moment – or so three of his subsequent vocal works suggest, with only the tiny Maeterlinck setting *Herzgewachse* (November 1911) reliving something of Op. 15's edgy restraint, as the text's reference to 'listless melancholy' prompts music of unusual calm and detachment. But that was after *Erwartung* had followed Op. 15's confinement of its mezzo-soprano to a chamber-music context with a terse psychodrama in which emotional restraint was abandoned as eagerly in the music as poetic discretion and balance were ousted from the text. Not all will agree, but it seems to me that Schoenberg's attempt to provide *Erwartung* with an operatic companion piece was a failure, an attempt at a drama with a more explicitly avant-garde character that seems to confirm that Schoenberg would never find an effective way of inhabiting such an ultra-modern world. Though *Die glückliche Hand* acquired some kudos during the later twentieth century as a post-Wagnerian, pre-Beckettian experiment in 'total theatre', it lacked input from both a professional librettist and a professional design artist; as the creator in total control, Schoenberg was simply too close, his experiences of life and art too raw, to do justice to his subject's dramatic potential. As an antidote to *Erwartung*, he might initially have imagined the kind of would-be redemptive sermonette that Goethe devised for the closing scene of *Faust* – as set boldly by Mahler in his Symphony No. 8 (first heard in 1910). The result in *Die glückliche Hand* is certainly modernistically heterogeneous to a fault, but its sketchiness is that of a sub-Strindbergian morality play, at best a trial run for some aspects of *Die Jakobsleiter* – which as it survives is unfinished but certainly not sketchy.

Jack Boss's analytical approach to *Erwartung* might initially inspire scepticism, given the exceptionally intricate graphics needed to present its findings. Yet it cannot be denied that

83

Example 4.5 Related settings of 'Ist hier jemand?' in *Erwartung*, bars 72–3

Schoenberg's pedagogically reinforced enthusiasm for traditional motivicism in music could not be entirely suppressed, even in a conception as dedicated to innovation as the monodrama. Commentators who use post-tonal terminology in their accounts of *Erwartung* can observe that, in a rare instance of traditional motivicism, Schoenberg's near-repetition of his four-note setting of 'Ist hier jemand?' in bars 72–3 can be thought of as two different versions of the [0134] tetrachord (Example 4.5). But this passage actually shows just how unwise it would be to allow the use of the term 'motif' here to encourage the assumption that Schoenberg was simply a disciple of Wagner writing music dramas against the still-relevant background of *Tristan* or *Parsifal*.

In Wagner, *Leitmotive* are not merely pervasive but prominent, their melodic character and explicit connections with characters, objects and ideas that fuel the progress of the drama and signal that progress to audiences who can learn, and often have learned, to 'read' what they hear and see. But with his unWagnerian flair for expressionistic concentration and disorientation, Schoenberg seeks a method and an experience closer to a psychoanalyst's probing of the patient's unconscious. Accordingly, he concentrates on the use of related and recurrent musical materials which are too brief or too closely welded into other no less salient materials to stand out in the way that the motives often proclaimed by Wagner in the boldest fashion at the very start of his music dramas stand out. So if, as Boss in particular has argued, *Erwartung* is a leitmotivic opera, it is one of a profoundly unWagnerian kind, and it becomes not only understandable but acceptable for commentators to argue with conviction for both apparently irreconcilable extremes – an opera without repetitions that is also an opera full of links and associations. With its simultaneously grasping for thematic consistency and rejection of melodically organised motivic writing after the fashion of Wagner or Strauss, *Erwartung* is surely Schoenberg's most avant-garde, even experimental work, a hymn to the night that is also a picture of night as curse and commination, something that threatened destruction to an artist bold enough to confront its most element aspects, and its most terrifying potential.

As mentioned above (pp. 74–5), near the end (bar 411) *Erwartung*'s protagonist reveals herself as a singer familiar with Schoenberg's 'Am Wegrand'. The song's extended tonality of D minor is hinted at in passing, but it is the melodic and harmonic focus on the three-note, major-minor third motif pitch-class set [014] that stands out in commentaries to a degree it can never quite manage in the actual score in performance, because it can never achieve the triumphant assertiveness of the great Wagnerian *Leitmotive*. The most celebrated of all those themes, the so-called 'redemption through love', or 'glorification of Brünnhilde', that ends *Götterdämmerung*, though forever transcendentally ambiguous in its meaning (beyond tonalities, chordal functions, etc.), leaves us in no doubt that for all its multivalence, it is supremely important. But in *Erwartung*, Schoenberg resolutely turns against such an upbeat affirmation of musical entities that build such decisive bridges between sounds and objects or ideas best expressed in words. As he might have said to Busoni in 1909, 'away with pathos, and especially when pathos is so explicit that it convinces listeners that they are consoled, and even healed, however profound their actual suffering in real life may have been'.

Notes

1. Bryan R. Simms, *The Atonal Music of Arnold Schoenberg 1908–1923* (New York: Oxford University Press, 2000), 89. Further page references in text.
2. Simms, *Atonal Music*, 89.
3. Simms, *Atonal Music*, 95. Further page references in text.
4. Julie Brown, *Schoenberg and Redemption* (Cambridge: Cambridge University Press, 2014), 150.

5. Seth Brodsky, *From 1989: Or European Music and the Modernist Unconscious* (Berkeley: University of California Press, 2017), 227–41.

6. Simms, *Atonal Music*, 94.

7. O. W. Neighbour, 'Schoenberg, Arnold' in *The New Grove Dictionary of Music and Musicians*, ed. Stanley Sadie and John Tyrrell, 2nd ed., vol. 22 (London: Macmillan, 2001), 589.

8. Walter Goehr and Alexander Goehr, 'Arnold Schönberg's Development towards the Twelve-Note System', in *European Music in the Twentieth Century*, ed. Howard Hartog, rev. ed. (Harmondsworth: Pelican Books, 1961), 88–106.

9. Jack Boss, '*Erwartung*, Op. 17: A Leitmotivic Opera and a "Cumulative Setting" Atomised', chapter 4 of *Schoenberg's Atonal Music, Musical Idea, Basic Image, and Specters of Tonal Function* (Cambridge: Cambridge University Press, 2019), 152–223.

10. For further discussion of this term, see Arnold Whittall, *The Cambridge Introduction to Serialism* (Cambridge: Cambridge University Press, 2008), 273.

11. Allen Forte, *The Structure of Atonal Music* (New Haven, CT: Yale University Press, 1973), 3. Further page references in text.

12. Arnold Schoenberg, 'Problems of Harmony' (1934), in *Style and Idea: Selected Writings*, ed. Leonard Stein, trans. Leo Black (London: Faber & Faber, 1975), 268–87 (284).

13. Forte, *Structure of Atonal Music*, 166–77.

14. See especially Carl Dahlhaus, *Schoenberg and the New Music*, trans. Derrick Puffett and Alfred Clayton (Cambridge: Cambridge University Press, 1989).

15. See Christopher Dromey, *The Pierrot Ensembles: Chronicle and Catalogue, 1912–2012* (London: Plumbago Books, 2012).

16. Glenn Watkins, *Proof through the Night: Music and the Great War* (Berkeley: University of California Press, 2003), 239.

17. Allen Shawn, *Arnold Schoenberg's Journey* (Cambridge, MA: Harvard University Press, 2002), 93. Further page references in text.

18. Bryan R. Simms, 'Whose Idea was *Erwartung*?', in *Constructive Dissonance: Arnold Schoenberg and the Transformation of Twentieth-Century Culture*, ed. Juliane Brand and Christopher Hailey (Berkeley: University of California Press, 1997), 100–8 (100).

19. Ethan Haimo, *Schoenberg's Transformation of Musical Language* (Cambridge: Cambridge University Press, 2006), 348.

20. Jack Boss, *Schoenberg's Atonal Music. Musical Idea, Basic Image, and Specters of Tonal Function* (Cambridge: Cambridge University Press, 2019), 152. Further page references in text.

21. For Schoenberg's letter to Busoni of 18 August 1909, see Joseph Auner, *A Schoenberg Reader: Documents of a Life* (New Haven, CT: Yale University Press, 2003), 70–1.

22. Arnold Schoenberg, *Theory of Harmony*, trans. Roy E. Carter (London: Faber & Faber, 1978), 418–19.

23. Boss, *Schoenberg's Atonal Music*, 165.

24. Goehr and Goehr, 'Arnold Schönberg's Development', 101.

25. Pierre Boulez, 'Arnold Schoenberg', in *Stocktakings from an Apprenticeship*, trans. Stephen Walsh (Oxford: Clarendon Press, 1991), 278–92 (283).

26. Pierre Boulez, 'Approaches to *Parsifal*', in *Orientations: Collected Writings*, ed. Jean-Jacques Nattiez, trans. Martin Cooper (London: Faber & Faber, 1986), 245–69.

27. Pierre Boulez, *Music Lessons: The Collège de France Lectures*, ed. and trans. Jonathan Dunsby, Jonathan Goldman and Arnold Whittall (London: Faber & Faber: 2018), 81.

28. Goehr and Goehr, 'Arnold Schönberg's Development', 102.

29. Alexander Goehr, *Finding the Key: Selected Writings*, ed. Derrick Puffett (London: Faber & Faber, 1988), 283–4.

30. Jim Samson, *Music in Transition* (London: Dent, 1977), 182 and citing Willi Reich, *Schoenberg: A Critical Biography*, trans. Leo Black (London: Longman, 1971), 54.

31. Daniel Albright, *Untwisting the Serpent: Modernism in Music, Literature, and Other Arts* (Chicago: Chicago University Press, 2000), 149. Further page references in text.

32. Allen Shawn, *Arnold Schoenberg's Journey* (Cambridge, MA: Harvard University Press, 2003), 96. Further page reference in text.

33. Brown, *Schoenberg and Redemption*, 151.

34. Arnold Schoenberg, *Selected Letters*, ed. Erwin Stein (London: Faber & Faber, 1964), 35–6.

AFTER *ERWARTUNG*

Fanatical Faith?

Writing a birth centenary tribute to Liszt in 1911, Schoenberg asserted that 'Liszt's importance lies in the one place where great men's importance can lie: in faith. Fanatical faith, of the kind that creates a radical distinction between normal men and those it impels. Normal men possess a conviction: the great man is *possessed* by faith.'[1] By then, Schoenberg was three years on from those months of maximum crisis and personal as well as creative turmoil in 1908–9 that had threatened to destroy his marriage just at the time when his most recent music was dividing his supporters from his opponents as never before. As states of mind, 'conviction' and 'faith' might seem to be synonyms, yet Schoenberg clearly wished to argue that fanaticism, being possessed (as it were involuntarily) by an overwhelming, compulsive conviction, was the one incontrovertible ingredient of greatness. He might well have claimed at that stage that the normality of conviction as the complacent embrace of convention was best exemplified in the world of contemporary composition by Richard Strauss. While the composer of *Elektra* might have been expected to approve of the composer of *Pelleas und Melisande* and even the second quartet, the incomprehension of the composer of *Der Rosenkavalier* when faced with the Op. 16 Pieces for Orchestra was entirely predictable. Yet Schoenberg's self-belief would surely have been shaken when he read in one of the last letters he received from Mahler that he too found Schoenberg's recent music hard to follow, as any composer as committed to the power of enriched yet ultimately resolving tonal harmony must surely have been. And if Mahler was undeniably 'great', where did that leave Schoenberg? It was as if the stronger his faith in the path he had chosen, the harder it was for others to distinguish faith from delusion; and pointing to such remarkable moments of harmonic affinity as the endings of

Gurrelieder and *Das Lied von der Erde* could not for a moment override the expressive disparity between the assertiveness of the former and the resignation of the latter.

Between 1899 and 1908, Schoenberg had put religious faith to one side; yet the realities of life with Mathilde at a time when he was struggling to establish a strong, personal voice as a composer and a strong personal following as a teacher seem to have left him increasingly dissatisfied with mundane, domestic affairs. Not for him the kind of contentment expressed by Strauss who, in beginning to plan his *Symphonia domestica* in 1903, had written of 'my wife, my child, my music/Nature and sun, these are my happiness', and identified by Charles Youmans with his 'post-metaphysical artistic practice'.[2] Bryan Simms has seen the matter of a shift from mundane to transcendental as follows: whereas Richard Dehmel's 'poetic language was direct and realistic … George is quite the opposite. In his verse every word hints at a transcendent state. The language is maximally compressed and devoid of either the mundane or the purely embellishing.'[3] A focus on compression and a retreat from the purely materialistic are evident in Schoenberg's response to George in Op. 10 and Op. 15, and when it came to planning ambitious works like *Die Jakobsleiter* and *Moses und Aron*, his pursuit of that 'transcendent state' – by way of his own texts – would be intensified. In 1909, however, with Pappenheim's collaboration, it was 'maximum compression' as an index of something unremittingly mundane yet also disturbingly intense, an individual, personal crisis that blotted out any sense of a higher purpose or of much if anything in the way of future prospects, that absorbed his creative energies. And even in later years, it would prove impossible to separate matters of religious faith from convictions about necessary compositional priorities.

Towards Unknowable Regions

It was in 1926 that Schoenberg published an essay baldly declaring that 'the only question is whether one can attain formal unity and self-sufficiency without using tonality'.[4] As a composer in the process of demonstrating how his newly devised twelve-tone method could be used consistently throughout a large-scale, four-movement wind quintet whose formal outlines were transparently those of classical tradition, and whose pitch relationships also acknowledged those traditions, though far less systematically, he may well have been more than usually impatient with the way in which words about music so arrogantly displayed their non-musicality, insisting on formulae that implied fundamental qualifications, like 'it depends what you mean by tonality', or 'it depends what you mean by formal unity and self-sufficiency'. There was something inherently non-conceptual about art – something metaphysical, transcending 'the realm of empirically founded, inductive science'.[5] According to the philosopher Rudolf Carnap, 'art is an adequate, metaphysics an inadequate means for the expression of a basic attitude towards life. ... Metaphysicians are musicians without musical ability'.[6] By the same token, musicians – composers, essentially, but also critics and musicologists – should find it hard to avoid everything metaphysical in working with the materials of music; and in Schoenberg's case, the fact that he took the materials of music so seriously, writing extensive texts seeking to explain their nature and use, signals a seriousness of approach that made it more likely than not that metaphysics, too, in relation to both music and his own life and practice, would exercise an increasingly strong hold over his creative thinking as time went by.

One of the most remarkable features of Schoenberg's life is that, at a time (1910–11) when he was transforming the nature of his compositional technique to reflect the radical effects of expressionism, and at the cost of inviting ridicule from most if not all mainstream composers and critics working alongside him, he should have spent so much time putting together a large-scale *Theory of Harmony*, 'learned', as his preface famously asserted, from pupils who shared his commitment to study traditional tonal techniques and forms while acknowledging the need to transcend if not contradict these techniques and forms in their original compositional work. Looking back on Schoenberg's later time as a university teacher in America, Claudio Spies made much of the difference between him and Paul Hindemith, teaching at Yale and notorious for a hands-on methodology that involved him radically rewriting compositional exercises that he found to be at fault, so that 'Hindemith's students rarely became sufficiently independent to avoid being branded with his particular notions of how composition "should be done". Nothing of the kind could be asserted about Schoenberg': there were no composition exercises in *Theory of Harmony*, and 'from Berg and Webern and on to Kirchner, Kim, or Cage, all composers who worked with Schoenberg went their own way. Schoenberg insisted on instilling in them all a feeling of indispensable independence and individuality of musical thought, as well as on each individual student's obligation to cultivate such independence'.[7] He taught composers, that is, but not 'composition', as individual, contemporary musical expression.

As James Wright argues, Schoenberg was convinced 'that composers must be liberated to manipulate the materials of music freely, in pursuit of whatever aesthetic goals they may envision. It is a position that weighs heavily in favour of the boundless capacity of the creative imagination and learned perception' (51), and demonstrated 'the delicate balance he maintains, throughout his theoretical writings, between a defence of "neutral facts" of harmonic theory and a dismissal of any kind of foundational aesthetic imperatives that purport to dictate the artistic ends towards which those facts must be employed' (56–7). Schoenberg's concentrated work on the *Theory of Harmony* may indeed have been influential in prompting the emergence of – in Wright's phrase – a kind of 'ontological mysticism' (96) that was the result of contemplating musical materials rather than any collection of sacred texts. Yet mysticism did not exclude an element of intransigence, as in his declaration of various aesthetic and technical principles in a letter to Busoni (August 1909), just before embarking on *Erwartung*, and including the bald injunction 'away with Pathos!'[8] From its context, it is clear that this injunction is far from advocating the rejection of all expressiveness and the embrace of a calculating, mathematical method of working that it can indicate in isolation. But Schoenberg's extreme radicalism in 1909 (not just in *Erwartung* but in Op. 11, No. 3 and the Op. 16 Pieces) should not be glossed over, since most other composers found it possible to treat disturbing subjects radically without jettisoning the sense of compassion and pathos that modernism had inherited from romanticism. In Bartók's *Bluebeard's Castle* (1911–12, 1918), another short, one-act opera, and close to

Erwartung in time, Bluebeard's recognition of the solitary dark-ness to which he has to return is part of a final scene that is essentially lyrical in character in a balanced melodic manner which the vocal line in *Erwartung* avoids. Consistently un-song-like, this resembles an extended recitative with short passages of more sustained arioso-like writing.

The reflective lyricism of Bartók's Bluebeard helps to explain the character's strange attractiveness to the successive women in his life, just as the Woman's fractured utterances in *Erwartung* graphically convey the immediacy of her despair. If Bluebeard's self-knowledge justifies the degree of sentiment inseparable from pathos, the Woman's state of breakdown may indeed inspire compassion in the observer – a compassion all the greater since she herself seems too disturbed to understand her own state. Given Schoenberg's situation when the work was written, it is difficult not to link its atmosphere to the idea of a wronged lover's revenge. But is the revenge that of a wife deserting/killing an unfaithful husband or the revenge of a wronged husband witnessing (and even welcoming) the mental collapse and abject humiliation of his erring wife? As one commen-tator succinctly concludes, 'neither Mathilde nor Schoenberg ever fully recovered from the marital crisis of 1908',[9] and Zemlinsky's biographer confirms that 'the "cloud" over the Schoenberg house-hold persisted for the intervening fifteen years between the Gerstl affair and Mathilde's death'.[10] When Zemlinsky finally conducted the opera's premiere in Prague, on 6 June 1924, it came just eight months after Mathilde's death, in her mid-forties.

Going Forward: From Miniatures (Op. 19) to Magnum Opus (*Die Jakobsleiter*)

In the year 2000, as the half-century since Schoenberg's death in September 1951 approached, David Schroeder wrote as follows:

A year after Gustav Mahler's death in 1911, Schoenberg had planned to write an enormous symphonic work in the tradition of Mahler. It was to have had four movements, each one based on a literary or philosophical text, using vocal soloists and chorus. The projected third movement ... with a pessimistic text written by Schoenberg, was to be followed by a finale with the solution to his philosophical and spiritual quandary entitled *Die Jakobsleiter*. The symphony never materialized, as it became increasingly clear to Schoenberg that he was not Mahler's musical heir, but completion of the fourth movement as an independent oratorio remained a high priority. Work on the text was under way as early as January 1915, and composition of the music began in mid-1917.

Schroeder then suggests that the completed text to this unfinished musical composition 'stands as a watershed for Schoenberg. ... Here he defined his spiritual objectives in composition in a new way, and at the same time took a large step in charting his future musical course and revealing the linkage between musical and spiritual matters'.[11]

There are many facets to Schroeder's explanation of the great change in Schoenberg's approach to composition, not least the perception that he was not, after all, 'Mahler's musical heir'. If heir means not just 'successor', but continuer and intensifier of comparable conceptions, this could well be true, although Schoenberg's emerging concern with 'spiritual objectives' in large-scale musical projects is hardly anti-Mahlerian. However, if, as is often argued, Schoenberg's earliest compositional tribute to the dead Mahler is the last of his Op. 19 Piano Pieces, written in May 1911, this certainly abstracts some very unMahler-like qualities from its muffled, tolling sonorities, together with the briefest of lamenting cries, stifled as soon as they break out.

The crisis years of 1907–9 had provided Schoenberg with ample opportunities to take refuge in Night Music. After the premieres of the Three Piano Pieces Op. 11 and *Das Buch der hängenden Gärten* in Vienna on 14 January 1910, the major music event of that year was a successful second performance of *Pelleas und Melisande* in Berlin on 8 October. But work on *Die glückliche Hand* moved slowly, and apart from the rapid completion of his treatise on harmony, with its feverish exploration of what progressiveness in harmony entailed, technically and temperamentally, Schoenberg focused on painting, with his first solo exhibition also in October 1910 in Vienna. The canvases confirmed that dark moods were still dominant,[12] and the incomplete state of the Three Pieces for Chamber Orchestra, which he worked on in February of that year, supports the general view that, apart from continuing financial problems, requiring a large loan from Mahler, questions of how to use his new ideas about harmonic organisation in ways which did not seem to be dependent on innovations initiated by Webern must also have exacerbated the problem. It might therefore be assumed that Schoenberg's eventual attempt to break out of this impotence, writing – or at least finalising – five short piano pieces in a single day (19 February 1911), by further focusing the turbulent expressionism of Op. 11, No. 3.

Far from it: the lurch into economy and spontaneity in Op. 19 is far from Webernian, but seems rather a response to the feeling that the challenge to comprehension represented by the 1908–9 compositions itself needed to be challenged, not by a retreat into old-style music but by a bolder delineation of innovative essences. What Jack Boss describes as 'the less-easily grasped procedures' of *Erwartung* and Op. 11, No. 3 contrast with the situation in Op. 19 where 'not only the motivic elements themselves but also their processes of development are quickly recognizable by the "naked ear"'. Because these pieces are so short 'there is much less room for motivic material that does not relate closely and directly to the main process. And another part is that these motivic processes are contained within miniature versions of recognizable tonal forms.'[13] Scholars may continue to offer different technical interpretations of how Schoenberg's notion of the Musical Idea is worked out in Op. 19, but the possible 'problems' which the pieces initially expose and the manner in which the music sets out to solve those problems can be explained and illustrated in a relatively straightforward manner. In No. 2, for example, Jack Boss and Matthew Arndt provide different takes on the music's use of suspended tonality and/or the modal aspects of 'extended common practice', but both agree that the 'problem' they identify (though different in each case) is indeed satisfactorily solved – resolved – at the end.[14] Op. 19, No. 2 is also a particular clear instance of a relative lightness of spirit: of the first five pieces, none is entirely dark and despairing, and to this extent they can be seen as marking the change of direction that would eventually find fulfilment in Schoenberg's determined engagement with metaphysics – spirituality – after 1912.

What changed between February and 17 June 1911, when the sixth piece was added, was seismic – the death of Mahler on 18 May. Given this context, one might a expect strong return of Night Music, and Boss implies a specific dark-side generic aspect: the sixth piece seems 'to portray Schoenberg's movement down and away from tonality as worthy of lament, whether appropriate or not'.[15] A descent is clearly the overall shape of Op. 19's last bar, but Boss emphasises the bar's tonally allusive pitch-class content to serve

> as a reminder of the piece's trajectory – the measure moves from V4/2 in E major to 6Z-12, a chromatic subset, on the second beat ... and then places a final emphasis on two WTo notes at the bottom.[16] In this way, the last measure leaves us with clear reminders of the visual and aural images that characterize Op. 19 No. 6 as well as its incomplete musical idea. The aural image consists of two bells tolling at Mahler's funeral, with Schoenberg lamenting his friend's death in between the bell sounds, through melodic outbursts of various kinds, some pained, some tender. The visual image adds to this picture, helping us to understand a second reason Schoenberg is lamenting: we see him (represented by the pitches in bars 3–4) reaching up to resolve in E major, to follow in Mahler's footsteps as a tonal composer, but his compulsion towards originality and the modern pushes him back down into chromaticism, pandiatonicism, whole-tone music, and his favourite hexatonic collection. (259–62)

Boss insists that, in the piece as a whole (Example 5.1), the technical 'problem' presented at the beginning, and elaborated thereafter, is never resolved, 'creating the incomplete musical idea' that leaves an impression of open-endedness. Schoenberg might indeed have been dramatising his regret, not simply at the loss of his mentor, but at his awareness that following in Mahler's footsteps (as he had arguably done as recently as July 1906 with the first Chamber Symphony's E major tonality) was no longer a realistic proposition. If, nevertheless, Op. 19, No. 6's first chord is sensed as a hazy reminiscence of a Mahler-derived motive (the Ninth Symphony's initial F sharp, A, B), it could then be argued that Schoenberg was acknowledging the gulf between Mahler's 'heavenly' E major resolution at the end of the Fourth Symphony and his own inability to resolve his profound lament into that unearthly key. As Deryck Cooke writes of the end of Mahler's Fourth, 'the sleigh-ride slows down in E major, for a final whispered statement of the main theme, which dies away in blissful murmurs: "There is no music on earth like ours; angelic voices ravish the senses; all things awake to joy"'[17] – as far from Schoenbergian realities as it is possible to be.

Example 5.1 Schoenberg, Six Little Piano Pieces Op. 19, No. 6

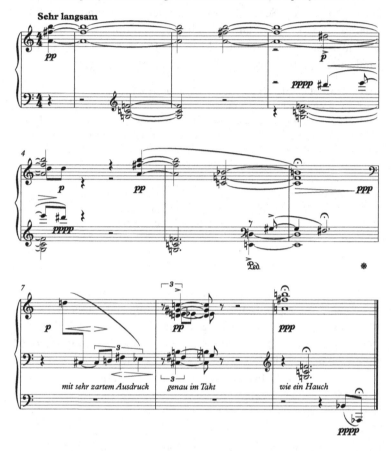

After 1911, the rest of Schoenberg's creative life would be
devoted to a creative context which Klara Móricz unsparingly
interprets as follows: a 'multidimensional but completely unified
musical space and his conception of a politically united Jewry are
two sides of a creativity inspired by utopian ideals',[18] for in her
view 'Schoenberg's conception of religion was nondenomina-
tional, tied to the abstract conception of his art'. As I have argued
elsewhere, however,[19] Móricz exaggerates the unambiguous utopianism of that 'completely unified musical space' and risks

distorting a Schoenberg whose innate and profoundly modernist aesthetic, embodied in his lifelong search for a viable suspended tonality – the difficulties of dealing with which are well illustrated in the writings of Matthew Arndt – acted as a counterweight to both spiritual arrogance and political intolerance.

With its invitingly sparse layout, Op. 19, No. 6 has been endlessly analysed, with interpretations ranging from those that prioritise ghostly hints of tonality to those that relish adumbrations of post-tonal systematics, as promised by the pair of trichords in the first bar, at once acknowledging and denying the siren-like lure of G major. Most strikingly, however, the piece seems like a Schoenbergian lament for a loss of confidence in building symphonic structures (instrumental or vocal) of Mahlerian substance and length in which convincing dramatisations of the endless struggle between the earthbound and the transcendent could be mounted. The giant symphony ending with *Die Jakobsleiter* may indeed have been conceived as a eulogy to all that Mahler had stood for in his symphonic music. But it was also a complement to Schoenberg's own 'evening-length' *Gurrelieder*; and if Mahler had lived for another year and a half, he might have been able to hear that work and decide for himself whether it sounded like the music of his uncontested heir. The trouble was, Schoenberg had not been writing music like *Gurrelieder* since about 1906, and the success of his giant cantata at its Viennese premiere loomed like a reproach over all the hard-fought technical and aesthetic battles he had fought over the intervening decade and would continue to fight, in driving his music away from late romanticism and towards unknown regions. In the end, nevertheless, Schoenberg's continuing struggle with the contradictory claims of Utopia and Dystopia – happy endings and exhausted collapses – might indeed have cast him, if not as Mahler's heir, then as someone permanently affected by the Mahlerian example he grew up with. After 1912, the alienation and despair, or else the fantasy of complete unity and serenity, detectable in the Night Music may have been pushed to one side; but it was never wholly eradicated. In Schoenberg, the shades of Night Music would never be completely erased, however strongly he tried to resist them.

The Dark Side of *Pierrot lunaire*

As argued earlier (p. 83), if Schoenberg hoped that – even more than *Erwartung – Die glückliche Hand* would achieve a perfectly realised form of genuinely radical operatic experience, the difficulties he had in completing the score indicate his struggle to bring such a heterogeneous yet highly compressed concept to a convincing conclusion. He was far more successful in the perfectly realised form of genuinely radical song-cycle experience that came with *Pierrot lunaire*. Written early in 1912 when *Die glückliche Hand* had been temporarily put aside, this replaces the soulfully lyrical mezzo-soprano of *Das Buch der hängenden Gärten* with a scarily volatile female clown (costume optional), whose archetypal comic-tragic shifts of mood and tone are made the more vivid by the composer's remarkable decision to replace singing lyricism with melodramatic 'speech-song', notated with flexible precision and creating choices for the performer that have been much debated down the years. Yet these issues have not prevented *Pierrot*'s regular performance and recording. Schoenberg's second radical decision in 1912 was to replace Op. 15's piano accompaniment with an instrumental quintet whose individual sonic qualities would be highlighted in a series of constant changes, no two successive movements having exactly the same accompanying ensemble. So although *Pierrot* has the same kind of overall design as a succession of short 'song' forms (twenty-one movements as against Op. 15's fifteen), it is often designated 'music theatre' rather than '(half-sung) song cycle'.

Apart from the obvious role of the 'Nacht' movement, it might be argued that *Pierrot lunaire* is macabre with sufficient consistency – even when the clown is affecting delicacy or sensitivity – to justify categorising the whole work as Night Music. After all, this Pierrot is affected by the moon, and only in the final stages do the chosen texts give any sign of interest in a sunnier environment. The last two movements even offer the prospect of happier times, with Pierrot on his return journey to Bergamo declaring that 'all of my gloom I've set aside / and from the sun-encircled window / I gladly view the lovely world'. But we know from the music that 'the ancient scent of fabled times' is a nostalgic fantasy of the kind that humans indulge in from time to time but never quite manage to realise in practice.

Seen in perspective, *Pierrot lunaire* is most radical in seeming to turn its back on those romantic song cycles that treat poetic introspection with the utmost seriousness – the kind of atmosphere so powerfully established in Schubert's *Die Winterreise* and reinforced nearly a century later in Schoenberg's *Das Buch der hängenden Gärten*, ending as it does with Stefan George's ominous description of the night as sultry and overcast ('Überwölkt und Schwul'). A collection of vocal pieces that is, for the most part, half-recited rather than sung and uses not just piano but an instrumental quintet for the accompaniment is clearly not seeking to proclaim close affinity with one of romanticism's 'signature' genres, and *Pierrot*'s sardonic, ironic tendencies are far from cognate with the romantic song cycle's characteristic blend of ardour and bitterness. For this reason – despite its frequently restrained and refined musical textures – *Pierrot* seems to invite the 'expressionist' label often assigned to it. And nowhere does that label seem more apt than in the eighth movement, 'Nacht'.

Any artwork featuring the moon in its title is likely to have 'something of the night' about it, as well as the potential for linking its imagery to lunacy. 'Nacht' (scored for female *Sprechstimme*, bass clarinet, cello and piano) does not actually mention the moon; instead, it speaks of what might be a lunatic's alarming fantasy, as giant black moths blot out the bright sunlight, creating a monstrous eclipse as the 'hearts of men on earth' are swathed in the blackest horror by such an intensely unnatural occurrence. The exceptional nature of this event is signified at an early stage by Schoenberg; he asks for the word 'verschwiegen' – suppressed, suspended – to be fully sung rather than half-sung, but to pitches well below normal female vocal register.

The entire musical commentary supplied by Schoenberg for this poem can be deemed ironic in that it complements the text's surreal horror with the time-honoured discipline of the form identified in the movement's title – 'Passacaglia'. But just as the music is not conventionally tonal, the form does not actually

Example 5.2 Schoenberg, *Pierrot lunaire* Op. 21, No. 8, 'Nacht', bar 10

provide the steadily repeating bass line familiar in passacaglias or chaconnes from times past. If the historical principle of the passacaglia is that because the genre-defining bass ensures the thematic essence of the piece, the upper parts can be more freely but still coherently constructed, Schoenberg's passacaglia is all-thematic in a modernist rather than classical sense; its basic motive – the 'head-motive', according to Joseph N. Straus[20] – is subject to a style of developing variation emphasising evolution rather than symmetry, so that the ending of the movement is quite different from the beginning. But there is no question that the principal motive throughout is the three-note setting of 'verschwiegen' – E, G, E flat [014 as a pitch-class set]: a bold musical paradox, the very sound of silence (Example 5.2). (It is of interest to note here that the last music Schoenberg penned in 1950–1, before lapsing into silence, setting the words 'Und trotzdem bete ich' – 'and yet I pray' – in the unfinished *Modern Psalm* Op. 56 c, uses pitch-classes G, B, E flat and C, a tetrachord including the [014] trichord, B, C, E flat.)

A sense that the basic disparity between musical notation and verbal language might be overridden – if only to the private satisfaction of composers – by transforming note sequences into personal names has always lent particular appeal to those names which can be transformed complete – as with Bach, Gade, Berg, Beach, Cage, Adès. When Alban Berg began his Chamber Concerto for piano, violin and thirteen wind instruments in 1924 – a suitably intricate and allusive fiftieth birthday gift for Schoenberg (completed and performed the following year), he prefaced the three-movement score with a motto theme in which Schoenberg, Webern and Berg himself were all portrayed by the translation of letters from their names into German musical notes.

If the Schoenberg cipher is reduced to six notes by the removal of the first-name letters A and D, it reads E flat (S), C, B (H), B flat (B), E and G, and during the mid-twentieth-century years, when post-tonal theorising was at its height, the idea was floated that, well before 1924, Schoenberg himself had appreciated the musical possibilities of such a 'signature' collection as a means of motivic self-identification – perhaps aware that his chosen [014] trichord in 'Nacht' could be extracted from the 'Schoenberg' signature hexachord [012569] – [014] = [125].

Once the prospect of fully or partially transforming significant words as well as names in this way is acknowledged – Schumann's 'ASCH' being an early romantic instance – new levels of speculative analysis soon emerge, all the more attractive for being ultimately unprovable as fact. For example, how likely is it that Schoenberg might not only have noted that three musical letters were shared by his own name and the word 'Nacht' – A, C, H – but also that he saw the possibility of cryptically associating his favoured 'night' motive – B, C, E flat – with the word 'Nachtmusik' (C, B, E flat or 'Es')? Although there has been considerable scepticism as to the possible rigour and extensiveness of such conscious calculations in Schoenberg's own music,[21] the undoubted prominence of this [014] trichord (as the conflation of a major and a minor third) in post-tonal and twelve-tone music has made it possible to interpret music like *Pierrot*'s 'Nacht' in terms of post-tonal or even pantonal invariants relating to a 'hexatonic' scale – in this case E flat, E, G, B flat, B, C – built from overlapping successions of major-minor trichords. The 'Nacht' passacaglia theme extending this motive is not at all like a twelve-tone series using only [014] trichords, not least in the obvious contrast between the leaps of its initial three notes and the semitone steps that succeed them (Example 5.3). But the eerie uniformity of the sunless dark imposed by those giant moths is memorably evoked by music so fixated on its own consistently dark yet far from immobile elements.

Example 5.3 Schoenberg, *Pierrot lunaire* Op. 21, No. 8, 'Nacht', bars 1–6

Musical Motives: Abstract or Expressive?

Although the issue does not feature in his discussion, Joseph Straus's decision to focus the first analytical section of his *Introduction to Post-Tonal Theory* on a brief comparison of Schoenberg's 'Nacht' with Webern's song, 'Wie bin ich froh!' (Op. 25, No. 1, written in 1935) serves to signal that identical post-tonal materials involving the pitch-class set [014] function equally well for Schoenberg's jet-black atmosphere and Webern's gently floating response to a poem beginning 'How happy I am!'.[22] Like all pitch-class sequences or scale segments, shorn of register, rhythm and any indications of expression, [014] can acquire any expressive aura the composer chooses to invent; it is not inherently, inevitably, sad or happy, dark or light. These two particular instances therefore cement the contrast between a composer often concerned with the psychology of human despair and one celebrating the natural world as, he believed, God's creation. Yet while Webern, fifty in 1935, was well established in his tendency, when choosing texts, to involve sacred, religious content, Schoenberg, in his late thirties in 1912, had thus far tended to prefer texts with relatively traditional romantic and erotic characteristics emphasising the solitariness and capacity for complex inner life of the human creative persona. True, the ecstatic, visionary outpouring at the climax of Stefan George's 'Entrückung' at the end of the String Quartet No. 2 appears to transcend mundane physicality and a purely secular ethos with the declaration that 'I am only a roaring of the holy voice'. But Schoenberg's own reference to 'the visionary poet . . . forgetting all the troubles of life on earth' does not extend into endorsing specifically religious associations of the kind discussed by Severine Neff;[23] and the movement's progress into the elegiac and purely instrumental coda, with its unsettling exchange between a minor and a major tonic chord at the very end, seems to signal that any repose after the rapture is tentative, even illusory. As for Schoenberg's slightly later George cycle, *Das Buch der hängenden Gärten*, the ending, as noted earlier, is in unambiguously earthly unease – 'Die Nacht ist überwölkt und Schwül' – 'the night is overcast and sultry': and the chord ending the instrumental postlude (shown as Example 3.2, p. 53) offers no certainty that the doubled bass note D is anything as stable as a tonic. Even if a D-tonality is heard as 'extended' rather than 'suspended' here, it is very far from the explicitly stabilising D minor cadences that end the orchestral tone poem *Pelleas und Melisande*, completed six years earlier in 1903. The downbeat atmosphere in all these endings – *Pelleas* as well as Op. 10 and Op. 15 – is a reaction, it might appear, to the serenely dappled coda of *Verklärte Nacht*; but, more directly, it is a prelude to the deeper darkness of *Erwartung* and 'Nacht' from *Pierrot lunaire*.

A Turning Point

Pierrot, as a whole, ends not so much in gloom as in hopeful uncertainty, the possibility that those 'ancient scents of far-off times' might actually turn out to be real rather than a drug-fuelled delusion. The work was first performed on 18 October 1912, just four months before the premiere of *Gurrelieder*, more than a decade in evolution, whose rapturous concluding hymn to the rising sun in the richest and most heroic C major (in the line of sunlit musical apotheoses like that of Wagner's *Siegfried*) did nothing to reduce a level of success that Schoenberg rarely experienced. Yet both *Gurrelieder* and *Pierrot* depended on texts and topics of a kind that Schoenberg would now turn away from. The likely reason for this has been succinctly diagnosed by William Benjamin: 'the development of Schoenberg's religious thought, in the direction of an uncompromising ethical monotheism, is paralleled by gradual changes in his approach to composition, in the direction of conscious, rational control of the creative process'.[24] And it is not necessary to counter Benjamin by arguing for giving priority to 'approach to composition' over 'uncompromising ethical monotheism'. The parallels between changes in ethos and changes in compositional technique were always evolving, always unstable, and while in general the years 1912–13 do indeed seem more like a watershed than any comparable time frame, it is obvious that there was not a sudden shift from all-pervading darkness to dazzling light in the tone of Schoenberg's music at that point.

In noting these changes, scholars have devoted much attention to another aspect of Schoenberg's affinity with Mahler – to put it awkwardly, the choice between Jewishness and Christianness. Early depictions of Schoenberg as an archetypal victim of prejudice that forced him to oscillate between Christian orthodoxy and Jewish commitment have been challenged, as the circumstances of forced exile and deracination have become distanced by time, and recently supplanted, or supplemented, by Klára Móricz's suggestion that his need for 'redemption' could only be met by creating 'his own religion'. Móricz links his transformational 'preoccupation with the striving for absolute freedom from material things . . .

from at least 1915, the time he began to work on *Die Jakobsleiter*';[25] and she is at pains to argue that, in her terms, even *Die Jakobsleiter* 'is not specifically Jewish in conception' (231). 'Like Balzac's, Schoenberg's spiritual quest was more of a transcendental endeavour than a religious pursuit' (300), and Móricz claims that only in the much later *Kol Nidre* (1938) – not a twelve-tone or even atonal work – did Schoenberg arrive at 'a surprising synthesis of presenting his religious and political convictions in a musical idiom that bears the composer's personal mark yet remains explicitly related to Jewish tradition' (252).

Móricz's stark assessment is expressed most directly in relation to Schoenberg's most ambitious attempt at a genuinely mainstream demonstration of twelve-tone spirituality, the unfinished opera *Moses und Aron*, begun in 1930. 'While strongly reminiscent of certain aspects of Judaism, the religious concept presented in the opera is nevertheless Schoenberg's own'; and so, 'the religion presented in *Moses und Aron* became Schoenberg's personal religion' (237). If this is true, Schoenberg's Moses-like isolation is powerfully exposed. Was he, in the end, the sole member of a community of one, his identity as expressed in his compositions truly unique? Or is it more realistic to propose that the particular tensions and topics contained in his work project a powerful social force to do with modernist struggles between the collective and the individual? With such issues predominant, it was understandable that musical characteristics related to the frankly mundane and often sinister attributes of Night Music should diminish, especially in those works that most fully embody Schoenberg's 'personal religion'. It can nevertheless also be argued that the technical features of Night Music, to the extent that these can be distinguished from its pictorial and textural elements, remained contributory compositional factors long after 1912.

Twelve-Tone Night Music?

In 1925, at the age of fifty-one, Arnold Schoenberg composed his *Four Pieces for Mixed Chorus* (Op. 27). Within two years of completing his first fully twelve-tone work, the Suite for Piano Op. 25, in June 1923, he had shown how the technique could function on the large, quasi-symphonic scale of the Wind Quintet Op. 26, completed in August 1924, and that same year – around the time of his marriage to his second wife, Gertrud, on 28 August and his fiftieth birthday on 13 September – he had travelled to Leipzig and Vienna for the long-delayed premieres of *Erwartung* and *Die glückliche Hand*. In April 1925, he had conducted a performance in Barcelona of another work from those pre-1914 years, *Pierrot lunaire*, and the strange, moonstruck spirit of *Pierrot* (1912) could well have been in his mind when he chose Hans Bethge's 'Mond und Menschen' (Moon and Mankind) and 'Der Wunsch der Liebhabers' (The Lover's Wish) as two of the texts for the Op. 27 choruses.

Bethge's German versions of Chinese poems are best known through Mahler's use of them in *Das Lied von der Erde* (1909), and 'Der Wunsch der Liebhabers' is not dissimilar in spirit to the lighter central movements of Mahler's song-symphony, evoking the 'sweet moonlight on the plum trees in the stillness of the night'. With its use of consonant, tonality-suggesting harmonies within what is nevertheless a twelve-tone texture, Schoenberg's setting sustains the convergence of older and newer elements that would prove so prominent in many of his serial compositions in the years ahead; and while the first two movements of Op. 27, using texts by Schoenberg himself, are much more intense and high-flown in their philosophical and spiritual associations, anticipating the often rather didactic manner of Schoenberg's later sacred compositions, the Bethge settings provide strong contrast. 'Mond und Menschen' might share a certain severity and sobriety with the first two Choruses; and the dancing rhythms and fluttering instrumental figures (for mandolin, clarinet, violin and cello) in 'Der Wunsch des Liebhabers', which echo the 'Dance Scene' from the *Serenade* Op. 24, have a slightly brittle quality that belies the text's serenity and calmness of spirit. But the overall effect is still far removed from the turbulent and predominantly dark, disturbed tone of Schoenberg's earlier 'music of the night' in its most fully realised and technically radical manifestations – in *Erwartung*, above all.

Postlude: Night Music as Prelude?

Arnold Schoenberg was a composer who lived through, and was greatly affected by, two supremely catastrophic events – World War I (1914–18) and World War II (1939–45). During the first, he laid the foundations for root-and-branch transformation of his approach to art in general and musical composition in particular, as a response to the need as he sensed it to establish a new role for spirituality in art, transcending the decadence and despair that had proved so productive in the years immediately before 1914 but now seemed limited and supremely negative. During and after World War II, contemplating the emerging information about the Holocaust from his American base, and doubtless appreciating that 'decadence and despair' in art is always paralleled by decadence in politics and despair in culture, he was involved in speculative planning for emigration and a possible administrative role in the new state of Israel, as well as in the creation of compositions that sought to encapsulate a kind of Utopian aesthetic by way of techniques that remained faithful to the modernist twelve-tone principles he had begun to employ around 1920, themselves a reaction to his own earlier, more overtly expressionistic modernism.

Though not excluding all commentary on the later Schoenberg, this handbook has been principally concerned with the music which preceded – and possibly provoked – that reaction: *Verklärte Nacht* and *Erwartung*, as well as the settings of Stefan George and *Pierrot lunaire*. Controversial when new, this body of work remains controversial today, since it embodies a paradox whose verbal explanation bedevilled Schoenberg himself for the rest of his life and continues to frustrate even his most recent explicators. As late as the 1940s, he could not avoid dramatising and justifying his principled radical moves half a century earlier as 'destroying tonality', fully aware that as soon as a more positive tone was attempted, the complexity of what was technically involved in transforming 'tonality' into 'pantonality' or 'suspended tonality' was impossible to explain in a widely accessible way. It seemed simpler and more effective to emphasise instead the 'idea' of varied development of basic thematic shapes as motives and melodies, presented within an appropriate harmonic context and thereby capable of achieving an aesthetic experience comparable to the clarity and coherence that instinctively satisfied listeners to classically tonal music.

No serious music historian has ever argued that Schoenberg's music after 1914 began to change in ways that soon left it with nothing whatever in common with his music before 1914. Naturally, the more detailed and specific the subject matter under historical scrutiny, the greater the scope for diversity of approach; readers curious for examples of this could begin by comparing chapter 3 from Ethan Haimo's *Schoenberg's Serial Odyssey: The Evolution of his Twelve-Tone Method, 1914–18*,[26] with chapter 9 of *Three Men of Letters: Arnold Schönberg, Alban Berg and Anton Webern, 1906–21* by Kathryn Puffett and Barbara Schingnitz.[27]

In his sixteen-page chapter, 'Before the Beginning. *Die Jakobsleiter* and Other Incomplete Compositions, 1914–18', Haimo focuses entirely on the evidence for the emergence of twelve-tone concepts and procedures in the various manuscript sketches and drafts which survive from those years, without needing to mention that there was a war on, or the impact of that war on Schoenberg's daily life. In their fifty-one-page chapter, starkly titled 'The War', Puffett and Schingnitz chronicle the daily life of the three composers by way of written correspondence that deals in great detail with the trials and tribulations of their attempted engagement with wartime events, leaving compositional considerations entirely out of account. Neither book sets out to provide a would-be complete historical picture of the composer as both creator and citizen in his time, and each in its very different way might be read as representing an authorial conviction that such aspirations to comprehensiveness and omniscience risk reducing complex contingencies to the simplistic fantasy of cause-and-effect narration. Any historian who steps away from the recitation of known facts into speculation about cause and effect does indeed risk implausible reductiveness; yet occasionally such a bold assertion of unqualified causality can ring true. It strains credibility to breaking point to suggest that Schoenberg emerged from his experience of World War I with a sudden, unanticipated certainty that the only way to continue as a composer was to reject his earlier technical and cultural preoccupations, closely connected as these were to Night Music, in favour of a way of composing suited to his revived convictions about the sacred and the transcendent. Rather, certainty continued to mingle with doubt, as it surely had from his earliest years, and his music continued to benefit from the strength of purpose with which he was able to give such forthright and eloquent expression in sound to these fundamental tensions.

Notes

1. Arnold Schoenberg, 'Franz Liszt's Work and Being' (1911), in *Style and Idea: Selected Writings*, ed. Leonard Stein, trans. Leo Black (London: Faber & Faber, 1975), 442–7 (442).
2. Charles Youmans, *Richard Strauss's Orchestral Music and the German Intellectual Tradition: The Philosophical Roots of Musical Modernism* (Bloomington: Indiana University Press, 2005), 229–30.
3. Bryan R. Simms, *The Atonal Music of Arnold Schoenberg, 1908–1923* (New York: Oxford University Press, 2000), 30.
4. Arnold Schoenberg, 'Opinion or Insight'? (1926), in *Style and Idea*, 258–64 (262).
5. James K. Wright, *Schoenberg, Wittgenstein, and the Vienna Circle* (Bern: Peter Lang, 2007), 31.
6. Wright, *Schoenberg*, 86.
7. Wright, *Schoenberg*, 83, citing Claudio Spies, 'Schoenberg's Influence on Composing in America', *Journal of the Arnold Schoenberg Institute* 19/2 (1996): 783–65. Further page references in text.
8. Joseph Auner, *A Schoenberg Reader: Documents from a Life* (New Haven, CT: Yale University Press, 2003), 70.
9. Alexander Carpenter, 'A Bridge to a New Life . . .', in *Schoenberg's Chamber Music, Schoenberg's World*, ed. James K. Wright and Alan M. Gillmor (New York: Pendragon Press, 2009, 25–36 (31).
10. Carpenter, 'Bridge', 31, citing Antony Beaumont, *Zemlinsky* (Ithaca, NY: Cornell University Press, 2000), 323.
11. David Schroeder, 'Arnold Schoenberg as Poet and Librettist', in *Political and Religious Ideas in the Works of Arnold Schoenberg*, ed. Charlotte M. Cross and Russell A. Berman (New York: Routledge, 2000), 41–2.

12. See Schoenberg's long letter to Berg of 31 October 1911 (*The Berg – Schoenberg Correspondence: Selected Letters*, ed. Juliane Brand, Christopher Hailey and Donald Harris (Basingstoke: Macmillan, 1987), 37–9.

13. Jack Boss, *Arnold Schoenberg's Atonal Music: Musical Idea, Basic Image, and Specters of Tonal Function* (Cambridge: Cambridge University Press, 2019), 227.

14. Boss, *Atonal Music*, 228–38; Matthew Arndt, *The Musical Thought and Spiritual Lives of Heinrich Schenker and Arnold Schoenberg* (Abingdon: Routledge, 2019), 193–6.

15. Boss, *Atonal Music*, 262.

16. For the six-note chord on the second beat, Boss refers to pc set 6-Z12 [012467: F/F sharp/G/A/B/C]. He then relates the last two notes – B flat/A flat – to 'WTo', the untransposed whole-tone scale C/D/E/G flat/A flat/C flat).

17. Deryck Cooke, *Guide to Mahler Symphonies* (London: BBC, 1960), 31.

18. Klára Móricz, *Jewish Identities: Nationalism, Racism, and Utopianism in Twentieth-Century Music* (Berkeley: University of California Press, 2008), 233.

19. Arnold Whittall, 'Metaphysical Materials: Schoenberg in Our Time', *Music Analysis* 35/3 (2015): 383–406.

20. Joseph N. Straus, *Introduction to Post-Tonal Theory* (Englefield Cliffs, NJ: Prentice-Hall, 1990), 23.

21. See especially Simms, *Atonal Music*, 80.

22. Straus, *Introduction*, 16–25.

23. Severine Neff, ed., *Arnold Schoenberg, The Second String Quartet in F sharp minor, Opus 10* (New York: Norton, 2006), 170–1.

24. William E. Benjamin, 'Abstract Polyphonies: The Music of Schoenberg's Nietzschean Moment', in *Political and Religious Ideas in the Works of Arnold Schoenberg*, ed. Charlotte M. Cross and Russell A. Berman (New York: Garland, 2000), 1–39 (1).

25. Klára Móricz, *Jewish Identities: Nationalism, Racism, and Utopianism in Twentieth-Century Music* (Berkeley: University of California Press, 2008), 230. Further page references in text.

26. Ethan Haimo, *Schoenberg's Serial Odyssey: The Evolution of his Twelve-Tone Method, 1914–18* (Cambridge: Cambridge University Press, 2006).

27. Kathryn Puffett and Barbara Schingnitz, *Three Men of Letters: Arnold Schönberg, Alban Berg and Anton Webern, 1906–21* (Vienna: Hollitzer Wischenschaftsverlag, 2020).

SELECT BIBLIOGRAPHY

Adorno, Theodor W. *Night Music: Essays on Music, 1920–1962*. Edited by Rolf Tiedemann. Translated by Wieland Hoban. Calcutta: Seagull Books, 2009.

Adorno, Theodor W. *Philosophy of New Music*. Translated by Robert Hullot-Kentor. Minneapolis: University of Minnesota Press, 2006.

Albright, Daniel. *Untwisting the Serpent: Modernism in Music, Literature, and Other Arts*. Chicago: University of Chicago Press, 2000.

Arndt, Matthew. *The Musical Thought and Spiritual Lives of Heinrich Schenker and Arnold Schoenberg*. London: Routledge, 2018.

Auner, Joseph. *A Schoenberg Reader: Documents of a Life*. New Haven, CT: Yale University Press, 2003.

Benjamin, William E. 'Abstract Polyphonies: The Music of Schoenberg's Nietzschean Moment'. In *Political and Religious Ideas in the Works of Arnold Schoenberg*. Edited by Charlotte M. Cross and Russell A. Berman. New York: Garland, 2000, 1–39.

Berg, Alban and Arnold Schoenberg. *The Berg–Schoenberg Correspondence: Selected Letters*. Edited by Juliane Brand, Christopher Hailey and Donald Harris. Basingstoke: Macmillan, 1987.

Boss, Jack. *Schoenberg's Atonal Music: Musical Idea, Basic Image, and Specters of Tonal Function*. Cambridge: Cambridge University Press, 2019.

Boss, Jack. *Schoenberg's Twelve-Tone Method: Symmetry and the Musical Idea*. Cambridge: Cambridge University Press, 2014.

Boulez, Pierre. *Orientations: Collected Writings*. Edited by Jean-Jacques Nattiez. Translated by Martin Cooper. London: Faber & Faber, 1986.

Boulez, Pierre. *Stocktakings from an Apprenticeship*. Translated by Stephen Walsh. Oxford: Clarendon Press, 1991.

Brinkmann, Reinhold and Christoph Wolff, eds. *Music of My Future: The Schoenberg Quartets and Trio*. Cambridge, MA: Harvard University Press, 2000.

Brodsky, Seth. *From 1989: Or European Music and the Modernist Unconscious*. Berkeley: University of California Press, 2017.

Brown, Julie. *Schoenberg and Redemption*. Cambridge: Cambridge University Press, 2014.

Bujić, Bojan. *Arnold Schoenberg*. New York: Phaidon, 2011.

Bujić, Bojan. *Arnold Schoenberg and Egon Wellesz: A Fraught Relationship*. London: Plumbago Books, 2020.

Select Bibliography

Cherlin, Michael. 'Pierrot Lunaire as Lunar Nexus'. *Music Analysis* 11/2 (2012): 176–215.

Cooke, Deryck. *Guide to Mahler's Symphonies*. London: BBC, 1960.

Cross, Charlotte M. and Russell A. Berman, eds. *Political and Religious Ideas in the Works of Arnold Schoenberg*. New York: Routledge, 2000.

Dahlhaus, Carl. *Schoenberg and the New Music*. Translated by Derrick Puffett and Alfred Clayton. Cambridge: Cambridge University Press, 1989.

Dromey, Christopher. *The Pierrot Ensembles: Chronicle and Catalogue, 1912–2012*. London: Plumbago Books, 2012.

Fitch, Lois. *Brian Ferneyhough*. Bristol: Intellect, 2013.

Forte, Allen. *The Structure of Atonal Music*. New Haven, CT: Yale University Press, 1973.

Frisch, Walter, ed. *Schoenberg and His World*. Princeton, NJ: Princeton University Press, 1999.

Frisch, Walter. *The Early Works of Arnold Schoenberg: 1891–1908*. Berkeley: University of California Press, 1993.

Gilloch, Graeme. *Walter Benjamin: Critical Constellations*. Cambridge: Polity Press, 2002.

Goehr, Alexander. *Finding the Key: Selected Writings*. Edited by Derrick Puffett. London: Faber & Faber, 1988.

Goehr, Walter and Alexander Goehr. *European Music in the Twentieth Century*. Revised ed. Edited by Howard Hartog. Harmondsworth: Pelican Books, 1961.

Hailey, Christopher. 'Musical Expressionism: The Search for Autonomy'. In *Expressionism Reassessed*. Edited by Shulamith Behr, David Fanning and Douglas Jarman. Manchester: Manchester University Press, 1993. 103–11.

Haimo, Ethan. *Schoenberg's Serial Odyssey: The Evolution of His Twelve-Tone Method, 1914–18*. Cambridge: Cambridge University Press, 2006.

Haimo, Ethan. *Schoenberg's Transformation of Musical Language*. Cambridge: Cambridge University Press, 2006.

Harrison, Daniel. *Pieces of Tradition: An Analysis of Contemporary Tonal Music*. New York: Oxford University Press, 2016.

Karnes, Kevin C. *A Kingdom Not of This World: Wagner, the Arts, and Utopian Visions in Fin-de- Siècle Vienna*. New York: Oxford University Press, 2013.

Markowitz, Mark D. *Alexander Zemlinsky: A Lyric Symphony*. Woodbridge: The Boydell Press, 2010.

Móricz, Klára. *Jewish Identities: Nationalism, Racism, and Utopianism in Twentieth-Century Music*. Berkeley: University of California Press, 2008.

Neff, Severine. 'Translation and Commentary'. In *Arnold Schoenberg, The Second String Quartet in F sharp minor, Opus 10*. Edited by Severine Neff. New York: Norton, 2006. 189–93.

Neighbour, O. W. 'Arnold Schoenberg'. In *The New Grove Dictionary of Music and Musicians*. Edited by Stanley Sadie and John Tyrrell, 2nd ed., vol. 22. London: Macmillan, 2001. 589.

Select Bibliography

Ogdon, Will. 'How Tonality Functions in Schoenberg's Opus 11, No. 1'. *Journal of the Arnold Schoenberg Institute* 5/1 (1981): 168–81.

Puffett, Kathryn and Barbara Schingnitz. *Three Men of Letters: Arnold Schönberg, Alban Berg and Anton Webern, 1906–21*. Vienna: Hollitzer Wischenschaftsverlag, 2020.

Samson, Jim. *Music in Transition*. London: Dent, 1977.

Shawn, Allen. *Arnold Schoenberg's Journey*. Cambridge, MA: Harvard University Press, 2002.

Schoenberg, Arnold. *Arnold Schoenberg Letters*. Edited by Erwin Stein. London: Faber & Faber, 1974.

Schoenberg, Arnold. 'Private Program for the First String Quartet (1904)'. In *Schoenberg's Program Notes and Musical Analyses*. Edited by J. Daniel Jenkins. New York: Oxford University Press, 2016. 151–3.

Schoenberg, Arnold. *Structural Functions of Harmony*, 2nd ed. Edited by Leonard Stein. New York: Norton, 1969.

Schoenberg, Arnold. *Style and Idea: Selected Writings*. Edited by Leonard Stein. Translated by Leo Black. London: Faber & Faber, 1975.

Schoenberg, Arnold. *The Musical Idea and the Logic, Technique, and Art of Its Presentation*. Edited and translated by Patricia Carpenter and Severine Neff. New York: Columbia University Press, 1995.

Schoenberg, Arnold. *Theory of Harmony*. Translated by Roy E. Carter. London: Faber & Faber, 1978.

Schoenberg, Randol, ed. *The Doctor Faustus Dossier*. Berkeley: University of California Press, 2018.

Simms, Bryan R. *The Atonal Music of Arnold Schoenberg, 1908–1923*. New York: Oxford University Press, 2000.

Simms, Bryan R. 'Whose Idea Was *Erwartung*?'. In *Constructive Dissonance: Arnold Schoenberg and the Transformation of Twentieth-Century Culture*. Edited by Juliane Brand and Christopher Hailey. Berkeley: University of California Press, 1997. 100–8.

Straus, Joseph N. *Introduction to Post-Tonal Theory*. Englefield Cliffs, NJ: Prentice-Hall, 1990.

Stuckenschmidt. H. H. *Arnold Schoenberg: His Life, World and Work*. Translated by Humphrey Searle. London: John Calder, 1977.

Vande Mortele, Steven. 'Murder, Trauma, and the Half-Diminished Seventh Chord in Schoenberg's "Song of the Wood Dove"'. *Music Theory Spectrum* 39/1 (2017): 66–82.

Vilain, Robert. 'Schoenberg and German Poetry'. In *Schoenberg and Words: The Modernist Years*. Edited by Charlotte M. Cross and Russell A. Berman. New York: Garland Publishing, 2000. 1–30.

Watkins, Glenn. *Proof Through the Night: Music and the Great War*. Berkeley: University of California Press, 2003.

Whittall, Arnold. 'Metaphysical Materials: Schoenberg in Our Time'. *Music Analysis* 35/3 (2015): 383–406.

Select Bibliography

Whittall, Arnold. *The Cambridge Introduction to Serialism*. Cambridge: Cambridge University Press, 2008.

Whittall, Arnold. 'Über die Anwendung der Musik auf das Drama'. In *The Cambridge Wagner Encyclopedia*. Edited by Nicholas Vazonyi. Cambridge: Cambridge University Press, 2013. 603–4.

Williams, Alastair. *New Music and the Claims of Modernity*. Aldershot: Ashgate, 1997.

Wright, James K. *Schoenberg, Wittgenstein, and the Vienna Circle*. Bern: Peter Lang, 2007.

Wright, James K. and Alan M. Gillmor, eds. *Schoenberg's Chamber Music, Schoenberg's World*. New York: Pendragon Press, 2009.

Youmans, Charles. *Richard Strauss's Orchestral Music and the German Intellectual Tradition: The Philosophical Roots of Musical Modernism*. Bloomington: Indiana University Press, 2005.

INDEX OF WORKS BY SCHOENBERG

GENERAL INDEX

General Index

General Index

General Index

119

Printed in the United States
by Baker & Taylor Publisher Services